"We love old tractors because old tractors have souls."
—Roger Welsch

100 Years *of*
Vintage Farm
Tractors

A Century of Tractor Tales and Heartwarming
Family Farm Memories

Michael Dregni, Editor
Foreword by Roger Welsch

With stories, photographs, and artwork from Bob Feller, Justin Isherwood,
Patricia Penton Leimbach, William Hazlett Upson, Ralph W. Sanders, Randy
Leffingwell, Andrew Morland, Walter Haskell Hinton, Charles Freitag,
Ben Logan, Bill Holm, Keith Baum, Jerry Apps, and more.

Voyageur Press
A TOWN SQUARE BOOK

Edited by Michael Dregni
Designed by Andrea Rud
Printed in Hong Kong

00 01 02 03 04   5 4 3 2 1

Library of Congress Cataloging-in-Publication Data
100 years of vintage farm tractors : a century of tractor tales and heartwarming family farm memories / Michael Dregni, editor ; foreword by Roger Welsch ; with stories, artwork, and photographs from Ronald Jager . . . [et al.].
        p. cm.
"A Town Square book."
ISBN 0-89658-462-3
    1. Farm tractors—United States—History. 2. Farm tractors—United States—Anecdotes. I. Title: One hundred years of vintage farm tractors. II. Dregni, Michael, 1961– III. Jager, Ronald.

S711.T476 2000
631.3'72'092273—dc21   99-042237

Published by Voyageur Press, Inc.
123 North Second Street, P.O. Box 338, Stillwater, MN 55082 U.S.A.
651-430-2210, fax 651-430-2211
books@voyageurpress.com
www.voyageurpress.com

Educators, fundraisers, premium and gift buyers, publicists, and marketing managers: Looking for creative products and new sales ideas? Voyageur Press books are available at special discounts when purchased in quantities, and special editions can be created to your specifications. For details contact the marketing department at 800-888-9653.

Permissions

Voyageur Press has made every effort to determine original sources and locate copyright holders of the materials in this book. Grateful acknowledgment is made to the writers, publishers, and agencies listed below for permission to reprint material copyrighted or controlled by them. Please bring to our attention any errors of fact, omission, or copyright.

"Working with Horses" by Ronald Jager from *Eighty Acres*. Copyright © 1990 by Ronald Jager. Reprinted by permission of Beacon Press.
"Allis-Chalmers and the Holy Grail" by Justin Isherwood from *The Farm West of Mars*. Copyright © 1988 by Justin Isherwood; revised text copyright © 1999 by Justin Isherwood. Reprinted by permission of the author.
"Iron" by Bruce Bair from *Good Land, or, My Life as a Farm Boy*. Copyright © 1997 by Bruce Bair. Reprinted by permission of Steerforth Press.
"Homemade Tractor" by Jerry Apps from *When Chores Were Done: Boyhood Stories*. Copyright © 1999 by Jerry Apps. Reprinted by permission of the author.
"Old Tractors Still Going Strong" by Frank Lessiter from *Centennial Farm*. Copyright © 1997 by Lessiter Publications, Inc. Reprinted by permission of Lessiter Publications, PO Box 624, Brookfield, WI 53008.
"The Harvest" by Jerry L. Twedt from *Growing Up in the 40s: Rural Reminiscences*. Copyright © 1994 by J. L. Twedt; copyright © 1996 by Iowa State University Press. Reprinted by permission of Iowa State University Press, Ames 50014.
"Rites of Passage" by Ben Logan from *The Land Remembers*. Copyright © 1975 by Ben T. Logan. Reprinted by permission of Frances Collins, Literary Agent.
"I'm a Natural Born Salesman" by William Hazlett Upson. Copyright © 1927, 1952 by William Hazlett Upson. Reprinted by permission of the University of Vermont.
"Another Dream Fulfilled" by Patricia Penton Leimbach. Copyright © 1977 by Patricia Penton Leimbach. Reprinted by permission of the author.
"Man Things" by Lauran Paine Jr. from *Man Things . . . Equal Time for Men*. Copyright © 1997 by Lauran Paine Jr. Reprinted by permission of the author.
"The Virgin on the Farmall—The Venus in the Chevy" by Bill Holm from *Landscape of Ghosts*. Copyright © 1993 by Bill Holm. Reprinted by permission of the author and Voyageur Press.
Doug Knutson's and Charles Freitag's paintings are reproduced by permission of the artists and Apple Creek Publishing, 101 Fisher Street, Hiawatha, IA 52233.

On the endpapers: *Threshing crew from a bygone era.*
On the frontispiece: *Happy farmers stand proudly before their handy Farmall tractor in 1940. (Photograph by Russell Lee/ Library of Congress)*
On the title pages: *International Harvester Farmall HV. Owner: Larry Eipers of Morris, Illinois. (Photograph by Andy Kraushaar)*
Inset on the title page: *A beaming farm boy takes his turn at the tractor wheel. (Photograph by J. C. Allen & Son)*
1910s: A tractor's helping hand
Page 6: *A Case internal-combustion-engined tractor provides power to the threshing machine in this colorful image from a classic Case brochure.*

Acknowledgments

I have been fortunate to work over the years with many of the writers and photographers whose essays and illustrations are collected together in this book. I would like to thank all of them as well as the others who helped make this book come to life: John O. Allen; Jerry Apps; Keith Baum; Tom Benda of Apple Creek Publishing; David Benson; Dike Blair; DeAnn M. Dankowski of the Minneapolis Institute of Arts; Bob Feller; Chip Fleischer of Steerforth Press; Charles Freitag; Connell B. Gallagher of the University of Vermont; Ken Gianini of the Minnesota State Fair; Bill Holm; Jerry Irwin; Justin Isherwood; Sherry Johnson of the Iowa State University Press; Andy Kraushaar; Randy Leffingwell; Patricia Penton Leimbach; Frank Lessiter; Andrew Morland; Lauran Paine Jr.; Robert N. Pripps; Ralph W. Sanders; Orlan and Mark Skare; and Roger Welsch.

1920s: Tried-and-true Farmall
Long days in the saddle of a mechanical mule were exhausting—but often better than long days walking behind a team of horses and a single-bottom sulky plow. (Library of Congress)

Contents

Foreword

By Roger Welsch

Roger Welsch's writings on tractors appear regularly in Successful Farming magazine's "Ageless Iron" section, as well as in Esquire, Smithsonian, and Nebraska Farmer. In addition, he is the author of more than twenty books, including Old Tractors and the Men Who Love Them and Busted Tractors and Rusty Knuckles.

 Rust? Iron? Junk? No, old tractors are a lot more than that. It's getting to be a tired word, but in the case of old tractors, "icon" is the most appropriate term I can think of.

I can direct visitors to maybe ten homes and farms within a few minutes of here where an old tractor is displayed proudly as . . . as . . . well, I guess as a lawn ornament, if not an icon. Some of them are painted up, most are simply old wrecks, hauled into place and left to rust as a symbol of something or another.

Now that I think about it, most of these old iron arrangements are more like shrines. It's not as if the machines are simply dumped somewhere around the yard. They are *placed*. They are in prominent view; they often stand on a pedestal or bed of clean gravel or rock; sometimes they are decorated (most often with lights, Santas, greens, and ribbons at winter); they are definitely more than plain ol' everyday yard iron.

What's that all about? Like most such phenomena, the last person to ask why some folks do this is someone who does this. They . . . *we* do this out of something so deep within our psyches that when asked, we flail for some kind of explanation for this peculiar behavior, whether it makes sense or not. "Uh, I just thought it would look nice." An old rusting hulk of a battered tractor because it *looks nice?!* No, I don't think so. "Well, my dad drove that machine the last fifteen years he farmed and so it kinda has sentimental value." And isn't that the same machine that broke his arm

twice, and aren't those dents in the hood from the time he beat it with an iron bar because it wouldn't start?! "I was thinking about restoring it some day so I thought I better drag it out of the woodlot before it completely disappeared in a pile of rust." Okay, that makes some sense.

But then we can ask the logical next question: Why do we *restore* old tractors? And that's a question I haven't been able to answer for my wife or, for that matter, myself, for seven years now. About once a month wife Linda ventures into my shop—almost always out of unavoidable necessity or to check to see if I am still alive. She waves aside the haze and smell, peers through the smoke and dirt, and shouts above the din, "So, this is fun, then, right?"

Yes, it's fun, but just like the lawn ornament iron, it's more than that too. Let's face it: There is *something* about old tractors.

An old tool becomes a favorite. You have a new Craftsman ⁹⁄₁₆ box-end wrench, and a fancy, screw-adjust low-profile jobbie your wife got you last Christmas. But for some reason you prefer the old battered wrench you got at a farm sale when you first started mechanicking. If asked, you might say that you prefer the old wrench because you know and appreciate its feel, because it has old-fashioned quality, because it seems to grip a little better . . . but ultimately, you like that old wrench better because . . . because you like it better. Because it's an old friend. And what would *you* rather do . . . meet a bunch of new people at a social

1937 John Deere Model A
A resurrected Johnny Popper waits proudly in front of a tobacco-drying barn. Owner: Dale Olson. (Photograph by Andy Kraushaar)

event and stand around making idle chatter or get together with old friends whom you can enjoy without saying much more than "Pass that popcorn over here, will you?" If you like old friends, you probably like old tractors. If you like old tractors, you probably like old friends.

I feel a little uneasy making this confession, but, in fact, sometimes old tractors are more than friends—they are kin! I once introduced Jan Jeffries, an old friend whose father's Allis-Chalmers WC was the very first tractor I ever owned and loved, as Sweet Allis's sister. Well, they both have the same father, Don Jeffries. And Jan did not deny the kinship.

Every time I have bought a tractor from an owner (as opposed to a salvage or junk yard) the owner has made it clear that this is not just old iron but an object of some affection and an item that is deserving of special attention and love. It's almost as if they want to make sure it is going to a good home. When Don Jeffries was ready to sell his Allis WD, he came to me. He knew I would treat this child of his as tenderly as I have Sweet Allis, and he knew they would sit side by side, just as they did for many years when they were part of his family, sitting side by side in his machine shed.

I know there are people who love their cars . . . automobile restorers, and all that. But I sure haven't ever felt the kind of affection for an automobile that I feel for tractors, nor have I ever met an owner who feels about a work-a-day car the way the way many of us feel about a thoroughly utilitarian tractor. In my case the contrast is even more dramatic: I don't like my cars very much. But I love my tractors. I have someone else change the oil in my cars; I rebuild my tractors from the bottom up, lovingly renewing each and every part. When I am asked about my Taurus, I can't even say with any confidence what year or model it is . . . 1991, I think, and, uh . . . an SE or SF or something like that. It's black—that's about all I know. I do know where the battery is, but I keep forgetting which side the gas cap is on.

1990s: "Evening Chores"

Looking back to simpler times down on the farm, this oil painting by artist Doug Knutson recalls the end of evening chores when it was finally time to park the John Deere in the shed after yet another day of hard work. A native Iowan, Knutson has devoted his painting skills to preserving Midwestern images. (Apple Creek Publishing)

Want to know about my tractors? Sweet Allis, my first tractor love, is a 1937 Allis-Chalmers WC, first tractor to come equipped with rubber tires. Like all Allises, it is Persian Orange. Its head bolts are torqued down to 70 foot/pounds on ½-inch stud bolts, 25 on ⅜-inchers. It has 19 horsepower, according to Nebraska Tractor Test #223. Original tires were diamond design Goodyears. It weighs about a ton and a half, give or take a few pounds of baling wire. That's not the original carburetor; the original was a Marvel-Shebler. That front screen is an after-sale addition too. The little flange along the front side rail is for the cornpicker. No, the little doodad along the shifter column to keep it from flopping wildly is not original equipment, but everyone who had an Allis WC had to add one sooner or later anyway, so it's dang near standard, if not factory. If you have the time, I could tell you a lot more about her engineering, stats, history, or character.

I bought my Taurus for $8,000; a friend gave me Sweet Allis.

Obviously I wouldn't have posed the question why we are so charmed by old tractors if I didn't have some idea about an answer. I think we love a good ol' tractor for the same reasons we love a good ol' dog, a good ol' wife, or a good ol' pair of boots. They are not complicated, and they don't pose a lot of unreasonable demands.

I come out of the house on a bitterly cold February day, powdery snow blowing around. I struggle to open the frozen garage door and clear away enough snow to get the car out. I unfreeze the lock and fold myself up to crawl into the front seat. I insert the key and turn it . . . rrrr . . . click click click . . . rrrrr. Nothing. It's a formality, but I open the hood anyway. I know there's a battery in there somewhere. Jeez, the engine isn't even lined up decently . . . in a tangle of hoses and wires it's *crossways*! I pound on the battery terminals with a pair of pliers, mostly to head off the inevitable command from wife or daughter to "DO SOMETHING!"

I'll call Al up at the garage in town to come down with cables and jumper it. Last time I did it on my own I burned out the computer, and it set me back almost $800 to get everything put back together again. This start-up will probably only cost me $20—unless we have to tow the blasted thing into town so he can warm it out and figure out what's wrong in the shop.

Maybe it's something as simple as a stuck choke, but I wouldn't know because I don't even know if there is a choke in there. I know there's not a carburetor. There's . . . something else. Grump grump, growl growl.

While I'm waiting, maybe I'll clear some of the snow out of the drive. I go out to the open machine shed and brush the snow off of Sweet Allis. No battery there . . . just four wires, one running to each spark plug. I pull the crank out of its wire hanger alongside the gas tank. I turn the choke lever down almost to the bottom but not all the way. She tends to flood if you turn it down all the way. I check the throttle and disengaged the clutch. (Even though I just pull the clutch pedal forward with my hand and set the iron catch to hold it, in my mind I know exactly what is happening inside the clutch housing because I have dismantled and reassembled a couple dozen WC clutches.) I put the crank on the front of the shaft, firm it up at the bottom so I can pull up and thereby avoid breaking my arm . . . or nose as has happened to some unfortunates. I make sure my thumb is on the same side as my hand, and pull up firmly. I can tell by the way it *feels* that it is going to start.

I step around to the left side again and let up on the choke a little. I give Sweet Allis an extra pat . . . I love her anyway, but in contrast with that evil black thing hulking in the garage and cursing my life, this morning she is a benefaction. I pull up on the crank and with an explosive, confident roar, yet once again for the hundred-thousandth time, Sweet Allis starts and is ready to do my bidding. No shoveling . . . I just drive her right through the drift in front of the shed. She doesn't care. She's my friend. If I want her to go through the snow drift, she'll go through the snow drift.

I break out the drive to the highway . . . and then I come back and make a dozen circles in front of the open garage door where sits the impotent automobile. When Al arrives, we jumper the car and it starts . . . it was just cold, maybe the battery was low. I drive Antonia to school and return the car to its cozy, dry garage. I slam its door and walk away with a silent curse. It's not that the Taurus is a bad car. In fact, it's much better than most. I'll admit it . . . I like my Taurus. It's just that, well . . . it's not a tractor. I *love* my tractor.

I start Sweet Allis again, drive her down to the river bottoms to see what's going on there, busting through

1900s: Good old days

An old-timer shows the new generation how the threshing operation works in this J. I. Case painting.

billowy drifts two feet deep, and then carefully park her back in her shed slot. As I stop her engine by shorting out the magneto, I pat her again with genuine affection and once again return to the house wondering how many times that engine has started up in her sixty-plus years, how many times those pistons have gone up and down, how many times I have patted her lovingly and gratefully. And how many times before me Don Jeffries did the same thing.

You don't feel that way or act that way with something that is nothing but old iron. No, we love old tractors because old tractors have souls.

Roger Welsch
Primrose Farm
Dannebrog, Nebraska

100 Years of Vintage Farm Tractors: A Love Story

Believe it or not, the book you are holding in your hands is a love story.

This is a collection of tales of undying adoration, testaments of faithful devotion, and sagas of enduring passion. It is a romance for the overalls-wearing, seed-cap-sporting, toothpick-chewing, oil-beneath-the-fingernails lover of farm tractors.

This book will stir your emotions, warm your heart, and spark your soul. It is a steamy potboiler—although ultimately it's devoted more to the gas-powered tractors that came into vogue in the 1910s than the early steamers of the late 1800s. It's full of wild passion—for Poppin' Johnnies and Minne-Mos, Farmalls and Fordsons. It will leave you breathless—over the quality of the restorations and paint jobs. It's a fantasy—as you dream of finding that coveted spoke-flywheel Deere Model D forgotten in an old-timer's barn. It's a bodice-buster—bursting with luscious photographs, tender portraits, enchanting artwork, and heartwarming stories about beloved standard-tread Oliver Super 77s, Allis-Chalmers WC row-crops, tracked Caterpillar Model Tens, Massey-Harris 101 Supers, wide-front Case VAC-13s, and Advance-Rumely OilPulls.

Some people who pick up this book may laugh at the idea of a tractor love story, but maybe they didn't grow up on a farm, or perhaps they are lovelorn themselves. The chivalry inspired by rescuing a tractor in distress is hard to explain to those who harbor no feelings for vintage iron. Surprisingly, many folk don't understand just what it's like to search scrapyards high and low for years and then, after you had given up all hope, to finally gaze upon the Holy Grail, a battered and forlorn Hart-Parr Model 30 radiator that will complete your restoration. Many never know the feeling of pride that comes from running your hand along the streamlined fender of your Minneapolis-Moline UDLX and hearing that 4.25x5.00-inch bore-and-stroke, overhead-valve, four-cylinder engine thump along like a heartbeat.

As the old saying goes, If it has to be explained, you probably wouldn't understand anyway.

A Century of Tractor Tales

This book celebrates one hundred years of our love affair with the farm tractor. It makes no pretense of being a true history of tractors full of important dates, essential facts, and details of model evolution. It is designed instead to be a history of tractors that is told in stories, as if you were sitting around the dinner table or the fireplace recollecting.

The stories have been organized by larger themes in tractor and farming history. These themes are events that have shaped the evolution of farming practices, the technical development of tractors, and the farmers' own lives.

1930s: Spring plowing
Springtime arrives, the bluebirds sing, pussy willows bloom, and farmers' thoughts turn to their tractors. This bucolic image was painted by Walter Haskell Hinton, a commercial artist from Illinois who crafted illustrations of tractors and farm life from the 1920s through the 1970s for Deere & Company brochures and calendars as well as farming magazine covers.

1990s: Amish threshing crew

A crew of Amish farmers thresh wheat the old-fashioned way. A Case tractor provides belt power to the threshing machine. (Photograph by Keith Baum)

The story begins with the creation of the first steam and later kerosene- and gasoline-powered tractors. These newfangled tractors symbolized the dawn of a revolution in farming—and were also a sign that a way of farm life was coming to an end. Old Dobbin's days were numbered when the first of these pioneering machines sputtered and coughed and kicked its way into life.

Yet just as the horse had been a partner in working the farm, the new tractor became almost like a part of the farm family. Farmers worked with their tractor from sunup to sundown, through rain, snow, and heat. Many families all but invited the Farmall to the table for supper.

These stories also recall home-brewed tractors that were fashioned by blacksmiths or farmers who were handy with a welding torch. Whether it was a tin lizzy converted to pull a plow or a homemade "Doodle Bug,"

as they were often affectionately known, these machines farmed countless acres over time.

There were also countless plantings, harvests, and threshings powered by tractors—as well as many hours spent on the old cast-iron tractor seat. All of these themes are discussed by the storytellers.

Today, vintage farm tractors may be ancient and obsolete, but through the hard work and busted knuckles of tractor restorers, the history lives on. Threshing bees, tractor shows, and farming museums keep the history of our agricultural past alive for future generations to help them understand the blood, sweat, and tears that built the family farm.

About the Contributors

The authors of the love stories gathered in this anthology include a Baseball Hall of Famer, a potato farmer, a former Holt Caterpillar serviceman, a former

1950s: Happy days on the farm
Sis and Junior take time out from their 4-H projects to frolic with Fido's pups while a Massey-Harris Pony tractor waits patiently in the background. This idyllic image graced the cover of a 1950s Massey-Harris Buyer's Guide.

International Harvester engineer, several famous novelists, and one farmwife. In addition, there are some stories by ordinary folk who simply love tractors and have a good yarn to tell.

Among the authors are Cleveland Indians fastballer and Caterpillar collector Bob Feller, writer and potato farmer Justin Isherwood, Wisconsin folk historian Jerry Apps, former Holt Caterpillar serviceman William Upson Hazlett, filmmaker Ben Logan, Iowa farm boy Jeffrey Twedt, former IHC engineer Orlan Skare, airplane pilot Lauran Paine Jr., prairie essayist Bill Holm, Ohio farmwife Patricia Penton Leimbach, Kansas farm boy Bruce Bair, and others.

The photography comes from a variety of well-known photographers and archives, including Ralph W. Sanders, Randy Leffingwell, Andrew Morland, Jerry Irwin, Keith Baum, and the magnificent record of American farm life found in the archives of J. C. Allen & Son.

In addition, there are paintings and other farm art from Charles Freitag, Doug Knutson, Walter Haskell Hinton, and more.

If you are one of the overall-wearing, seed-cap-sporting, toothpick-chewing, oil-beneath-the-fingernails lovers of farm tractors, this romance is for you.

Chapter 1

The Coming of the Iron Horse

*"The horse and man made civilization: they should
forever stand inseparable."*
—The Horse Association of America's *1924 Annual Report* warning
against the rising spectre of farm tractors

From the late 1800s through the 1940s, a war was fought on American soil. The war cast the time-honored methods of farming with a team of horses against the newfangled concept of a tractor. The battles were bitter, waged in agricultural magazines, in county extension bulletins, and in fields with neighbors pitted against each other over the issue of horse power versus horsepower.

From the 1920s, tractors were refined, and the horse's days down on the farm were numbered. Ultimately, the tractor won the war, and many a farmer bade a sad farewell to Old Dobbin as the horse was traded in on a Farmall or a Johnny Popper.

1940s: Feeding the mechanical mule
Main photo: *A farm boy gases up the family Farmall. As tractor salesmen liked to tell those potential customers who stuck with their horse teams, the iron horse only eats when it's working. (Photograph by John Vachon/Library of Congress)*

1920s: Case brochure
Inset: *A new day was dawning on the farm with the arrival of the iron horse.*

Working with Horses

By Ronald Jager

Ronald Jager came of age on an eighty-acre farm in Missaukee County, Michigan. As he writes in his memoir of that farm upbringing, *Eighty Acres: Elegy for a Family Farm*, "There we, a family of seven, worked hard, played hard, felt the pungency of farm life. It will be a part of us all forever."

While Jager's writing is nostalgic, it is also realistic. Life on the farm, even looking back on the golden days of his childhood, was not all playing in the hayloft or galloping horses around the acreage. Jager notes in his preface, "My aim in this book is documentary: to capture and exhibit the experience of being young and on a farm—work and whimsy, warts and all."

This chapter on working with horses is Jager's eulogy to the way of farming—and the way of *life*—that he grew up with but saw passing as the mechanical mule replaced the horse of flesh and blood.

Driving a team of horses is a basic, gentle pleasure, especially flattering to a farm boy's self-image. Draft horses are large and mighty creatures, clumsy, usually patient, without much personality, and fairly easy to control if they don't get any surprises. Surprised horses sometimes create memorable experiences. One of the most emphatic lessons my father taught his sons was this: Never get within kicking range of a horse without speaking to it; let the horse know you are there. And none of us ever got kicked by a startled horse. Operating some implements, such as binders and plows, required certain advanced skills and cautions, but handling the team was the easy part. The horses knew what job they were doing, they knew the way to carry the sleigh, and they picked up quickly on the dull fact that they should follow the furrows, the rows, the ruts, walk slowly, turn around at the end, stand, or whatever.

For my brothers and me the first real job with horses—at about age ten—was "driving in front of the loader." This early exercise of horsemanship is vital nourishment to a farm boy's hungry ego. He rides out to the field on the hay wagon with two men, leaning as they do on a pitchfork to steady himself as the horses amble down the lane to the back forty. He is now an intimate part of the working realities of farming and he suddenly realizes—gazing appreciatively at his shadow as it whips over the grass and past the fence posts—what a striking figure he cuts, standing there on the wagon, fork in hand, stalwart as a man among men.

The hay has been cut, wilted for a day, then raked

1990s: Working the team
An Old Order Amish farmer tends his cornfield with a team of three mules in Lancaster County, Pennsylvania. While working with horse, mule, or oxen teams is a way of the past on most North American farms, Amish and farmers from other religious beliefs still swear by them. (Photograph by Keith Baum)

into windrows so that it is bunched sufficiently for the hay loader to pick it up automatically. We hitch the hay loader to the rear of the wagon, and the horses amble slowly down the windrow of hay, one on either side, the wagon straddling the hay, which is picked up by the loader and rolled onto the wagon. The horses have the bit in their teeth and they know exactly what is expected of them. Young and spirited horses will sense that the boy's tug on the reins and the voice at the end of them lack authority, and that sometimes prompts them to ignore the driver; they might simply turn and head for the barn. Veteran horses are more predictable, merely stopping now and then to munch hay and to see if anybody is paying attention.

The loader sweeps up the hay in a long unbroken roll and dumps it gently on the back of the wagon, where two men, movements synchronized, begin to build the load. Up front our boy-man drives the horses. That is to say, he holds the lines (*reins* was a book word, *lines* was a farm word), giving it his full attention; and as the load mounts he climbs aloft on the ladder attached to the wagon's front. The higher the load the higher the honor. At last the driver-hero is nestled against the topmost rung of the ladder, a ton of hay beneath him, hay piled high around him, wisps of hay poking him in the neck. The views from this elevation are exciting: down there are the raspberry bushes, the stone piles, the long fencerows, and there beneath him too are the broad, sweating backs of the horses, still obedient to his every command. Through the lines he can telegraph wordless instructions down to them: a sharp tug ("Whoa!") or a gentle flipping ("Geddup!"); or he can turn the whole vast procession, horses and wagon and loader (sharp "Gee"), to begin a new windrow. A man's world.

The load completed, he relinquishes the lines at last to one of the other men for the triumphant trip back to the barn. Past the apple orchard and into the lane they go, gliding, riding at treetop level on a gentle cushion of twelve feet of packed hay. Would that someone nearby had a camera!

Even before Nelvin and I were old enough to drive the team, we sometimes hitched a ride home to the barn on the hay load. We got permission to climb the tall ladder, scrambled to the top, and settled into the soft and prickly hay beside Marvin, who had been the driver. One day, Ben Baas, a neighbor with whom we

exchanged work during haying season, was to drive home the load, and my father was walking. Just as we started out, one of the horses' lines got caught under the front of the wagon tongue. (The tongue is a long tapered pole connected to the front axle so as to command the steering of the wagon; about five inches in diameter, it runs between the horses and is fastened and upheld at the horses' chest.) The tangled line was a minor detail, but we had to correct it before proceeding, and Ben climbed down the wagon ladder at the front of the load. Instead of going to the ground and walking around, he stepped out on the tongue between the horses to reach for the tangled line. That's the kind of shortcut a farmer might take with his own team, not often with someone else's. These were our horses, not Ben's, and they were startled by this unfamiliar approach and they jumped. When Ben tried to calm them from his precarious position on the tongue, they panicked and broke into a trot. He grabbed the harness hames, and as the horses picked up speed and headed for a hillside, he hung on for his life—literally, for he was standing on the tongue between the runaway horses, and if he had fallen he would have been trampled and run over.

We who were on top of the load had an unexpected ride, very short and swift; for a load of hay is not made for high-speed turns on hillsides, and this one didn't survive it. The hay did not slide off—it flipped off, downhill side, and landed upside down like a pancake. We three boys sailed through the air, crash-landed headfirst, and were simultaneously buried under a ton of hay. Nelvin and I were stunned and helplessly pinned down, faces buried in the stubble. I remember being unable to move at all, then eventually hearing Marvin's voice calling me, very faintly and far away, but being unable to answer. In fact, he was only ten feet away; he had pushed himself clear and was digging and calling for us.

Nearby, Ben was getting the ride of a lifetime astride a narrow wagon tongue between a runaway team cutting hillside capers. Eventually he grabbed one line and turned the horses and their empty wagon in sharp circles until they calmed down. By then, my father was on a dead run from the barn back to the field, and Marvin was digging for his little brothers in the pile of hay. He got a grip on my left hand and dragged me out into the sunlight, spitting chaff and panic; and just as he did so he answered Dad's call by shouting that,

1920s: Farming the old-fashioned way

A farmer steers his team in this painting by famed farming artist Walter Haskell Hinton. When the first lightweight farm tractors arrived in dealer showrooms in the 1910s and 1920s, it was this type of farmer who was the sales target. As Ford-Ferguson 9N designer and engineer Harold Brock remembered, "Our competition was not other tractor brands. We felt our competition, at least back in 1938, was the horse."

CITY FOLKS JUST DON'T GET THE SAME AIR WE DO!

1920s: Postcard humor

While exhaust fumes were an issue whether you had a team or a tractor, many farmers who swore by their horses also proclaimed that tractors would be the ruination of the power farmer because the machines didn't produce that essential byproduct, manure.

yes, we were all right. I bellowed after him that we were not all right. Marvin commanded me to pipe down and help to find Nelvin. Then he dived back under the hay and came back tugging a leg, this time with Nelvin attached.

We weren't really hurt much, just bruises and scratches aggravated by hysteria. My mother's therapy for the situation, very successful indeed, was threefold: salve for our sores; sage tea, a favorite beverage, for our stomachs; and then to bed on the sofa with the shades drawn. By suppertime we were in good repair again. The next day we were ready to go back to haying.

A plow is a very simple device—basic, precise, and unimaginably ancient. Although farming is not a graceful business, plowing with horses comes close: no gears, no clatter or clutter, only the throaty murmur of the plowshare and the elegant ripples of the furrows across the scenic fields. Some scents of the countryside are sweeter than a new-made furrow, but the smell of the fresh, moist earth represents elemental things. Farmers have ever found an earthy pleasure in turning over the soil with a plow, found a satisfaction in its quiet Precision and calm, such as cannot be found in haying or harrowing, in sowing or reaping. I sensed something of that already when I was a five-year-old fanatic, following in the furrows behind my father's plow, hour after hour.

I have read that in some parishes in England, Plough Monday (first Monday after Epiphany) and a

service of Blessing the Plough are still observed, in a tradition harking back to medieval Ploughman's guilds. Even secular farmers who have never heard of it would understand that. The senses and the symbols all agree: the first plowman was the first farmer.

Plowing demands considerable strength and skill, and plowing a straight furrow with horses requires quick reflexes, a good eye, and much practice. (What advantage has a straight furrow over a crooked one? Practically speaking, none at all. That is why it is so important.) My father did not teach his sons to plow. He had reasons: there was not a lot of plowing to be done; it was a skill we might not need later in life; he knew we would botch the job with sloppy, crooked furrows, painful to look at; he enjoyed doing the plowing himself. By the time we were strong enough to handle the plow behind the horses, we were already working for the neighbors, plowing crooked furrows with their tractors—an arrangement that satisfied everybody.

Tractor engines have reduced the melodies of farming to a low common denominator, for they sound essentially the same whatever work they are doing, whereas each horse-drawn farm implement makes its own individual country music, its own sensual claims on memory. The cultipacker clatters and clunks and clangs, its heavy iron packers bumping each other as they roll over and compact the soil lately sown to grain. Whereas the harrow is as silent as a plow, the binder is a big bandwagon of noise, of cutting and whirring, of rattling and churning. But the binder's sounds don't carry far; the much gentler rattle of the horse-drawn mowing machine drifts farther across the fields. A half mile away the mower's sound is a steady rhythmic hum, resolving, as it draws near, into a smooth clatter, almost a purr, the prim sound of efficiency. When sounds of mowers come, can fragrances of new-mown hay be far behind?

In a class by itself for the production of sheer unmitigated country racket is the threshing machine. This monster specializes in sensory overload. Once a year it tramped through our neighborhood, noisily devouring stacks of grain, emitting bags of wheat and oats, and spitting straw into large scenic heaps. Threshing day was always a major event: lots of sound and fury, signifying everything, beloved of children. On that day tractors and horses, wagons and neighbors descended on the farm, all in high spirits. When we were very young, Nelvin and I would scramble up to a precarious high beam in the barn far above the threshing floor and perch there to watch the annual pageant below. Gingerly we slid out along the beam to secure bits of dried sparrow dung to drop down on the threshers, scoring a bull's-eye just in time to gaze innocently in another direction.

When we were older we maneuvered to be assigned to drive a tractor and wagon (not a team and wagon, because a team owner seldom assigned horses to a stranger; tractors were not so fastidious) to haul the loads of grain from the field to the waiting threshing machine. When we were still older, someone younger drove the tractor and we handled a pitchfork with the rest of the crew. For a brief period in the late forties, horses and tractors often worked side by side bringing in grain from the fields on threshing day, but the general commotion associated with threshing was not congenial to horses, and that itself often provoked new installments of the ongoing horse-versus-tractor debate. We had a young cousin who actually preferred driving horses to driving a tractor—a disgrace to his generation.

A cultivator is a simple one-horse implement with plowlike handles and half a dozen shovels to stir the soil and uproot the weeds between the rows of crops. With it you can cultivate corn long after it is too tall to run through with a tractor cultivator; you can also use it when the fields are too wet to bear a tractor's weight.

(Score that for the horse; and add that horses never get stuck.) Moreover, a boy can operate a cultivator as soon as he has strength to steer the thing and hold it upright. Perhaps he is only twelve or thirteen years old, but if he can do it at all he can do as much as a man in a day, for the horse determines the pace. Both hands are needed on the handles, however, so the operator loops the lines around his back and has to twist his body left and right to apply pressure on the horse's bit. It sounds more difficult than it is. If either the boy or the horse is experienced, cultivating is a simple job and, to my mind at least, far more satisfying than hoeing.

One day Marvin was cultivating the corn south of the woods, Dad was cultivating beans in the opposite corner of the farm, and Nelvin and I, too young for this work, were engaged in a favorite pastime: building shacks of sticks and leaves in the woods. Deciding to take a break, Marvin parked the cultivator and his horse, Pearl, at the edge of the field and came to see what we were up to in the woods. It must have looked all right to him, for very soon all three of us were deep into the design and construction of a new and improved leaf-and-stick shack.

Pearl was normally a patient beast, but she became bored with the delay and decided to strike out for home. Unseen by us she started down the corn row; the cultivator flipped over; she mowed corn all the way to the end. For a full quarter of a mile Pearl never deviated, and thus very neatly and precisely flattened two entire rows of corn every blessed hill. She might have reversed course at that point, as she had been doing all morning, and mowed another set of rows, but she didn't. She took a right turn, got to the lane, took a left, and made straight for the stable. Having arrived there, she had to become resourceful to get in: some stupid contraption seemed to be dragging behind her, something that just wouldn't fit through the door. As was her wont, Pearl just backed off and calmly took a couple of hard lunges until she had wiped off the offending thing, widening the door somewhat in the process. Horses are not gentle creatures, so she left pieces of her harness there, too.

Meanwhile, back at the shack in the woods, we three were having a great time. But eventually we decided to lay off architecture and return to farming. Let's see now—where was Pearl again? All we could find in the cornfield was a very eloquent trail of evidence, leading inexorably to the barn door. At the door, various bits of harness, doorjamb, and cultivator told us all we needed to know and much more than we wanted to. Pearl was in her proper stall munching hay, not a care in the world. Oh, to be a horse! Nelvin and I helped Marvin pick up the pieces, but when Dad came in from his corner of the farm, we quietly absented ourselves from the proceedings.

Plowing is regularly followed by harrowing, which is aimed at breaking up the sod chunks, leveling the field, loosening the soil, and preparing it for planting. Each field is harrowed at least twice before the seed is put in. When the seed was grain, which my father always broadcast by hand because he didn't own a grain drill and liked sowing by hand, then the field was worked a third time to "harrow the seed under." Harrowing does not require much skill. It lacks the precision and definiteness of plowing, and doesn't have the historic symbolism of plowing, either. Harrowing is banal enough so that it's hard to perform badly; and nobody ever devised a service of Blessing the Harrow. Even for horses it is easy work, but I presume horses with dignity are bored by it. The horse-drawn harrow was pretty well standardized centuries ago: it has four steel runners and several dozen spring-steel tines, each two and a half inches wide, which can be adjusted for depth. With this elementary contraption and a team of horses, a young man can, on his very first dash across the field, do the job just about as well as anyone ever will.

However, there is one serious mistake that can be made with a harrow.

When you reverse direction at the edge of the field, you can make too sharp a U-turn, and the results can be spectacular. Many a farm boy has grown to manhood, I'll bet, without knowing exactly what would happen if he were to make that mistake. I am not so innocent. On a normal turnaround the harrow simply slides around on the ground, the outside runner doing a semicircle as it revolves around the inside runner, which pivots in place. However, the harrow is designed to flex or fold at the center—like a face-down open book—to accommodate itself to uneven ground; and if you turn too sharply the harrow rides too heavily on its inside runner, rises and flexes at the center, and drags the outside runner underneath it. (Push a face-down open book against something: it will rise

---

These Newfangled Machines
By Toivo Anderson of Calgary, Alberta

The horsemen that were raising horses and breeding them for sale didn't like it at all when tractors first came in. They felt that they could get out on the land when the conditions weren't just right for tractors. Well, they might have had soil that worked when it was wetter, but most of the time soil has to be just right to work at any time, with any machine. And of course the tractor man, he used to point out that his motive power didn't need anything to eat while it was standing idle, and the horsemen, they even went as far as to figure out the cost of feeding a horse over winter.

The horsemen felt that it wasn't fair that they were being put out of business by these newfangled machines that were coming in, like gas tractors. They said, with gasoline at thirty cents a gallon, it wasn't economical, and the home-grown fuel for the horses was better— but they had to feed the horses over winter when they weren't even worked.

---

up, snap closed, and flip over. So will a harrow!) At this point the harrower must react with lightning speed to keep the harrow from folding and flipping like a book. As with many farm jobs, the driver suddenly needs four hands: two to grip the reins to straighten out the horses, and two to yank the harrow back into its normal flat position.

The day I lost my innocence I dropped a line while making a desperate lunge for the tipping harrow. The horses cranked around in too sharp a turn, and the harrow rode up on its edge, started to flip, and frightened the horses. At that we all rapidly descended into a state of churning chaos. Panicked, the horses went into a brisk circling maneuver, kicking over the traces, snorting, then jumping, dragging the harrow in bouncing circles—a crazy dervish dance that scared me witless. Tugging at the one line I still held and shouting, I tried to keep out of the path of the spinning cyclone of horseflesh, field dust, and flying harrow. How would I ever stop this ghastly dance? No way. I could not stop it.

It just stopped. Precisely at that moment an angel appeared at my side. He was oddly disguised as a truck

A. Fletcher's threshing outfit on D Coheland's farm, Oct. 1905.

1900s: Modern times
Modern all the way, this Canadian farm might still have an outhouse, but a brand-new Case steam engine had replaced the old-fashioned rotating horse power in driving the threshing machine. Horse teams were now relegated to the supporting role of hauling wagons to feed the threshing outfit. (Glenbow Archives)

driver who had seen a boy in trouble in a field, stopped, alighted, and strode over. He calmly helped me untangle horses, harrow, and harness. "The funniest things can happen with horses," he said. That's exactly what he said! I was staggering from terror and adrenaline overdose, and he thought this was *funny*? Evidently, angels have a weird perspective on reality. The harrow, having been through some very unharrowlike maneuvers, had a, well, funny shape. But what was so funny about that? Even the horses, Pearl and Barney, were trembling, their great heaving sweating bodies shaking like quaking aspen leaves; they did not seem amused to me. It would take me years to find the funniness. I thanked the obliging stranger, who disappeared into a cloud (dust, I suppose), I rehitched the horses to what had been a harrow, compensating as well as I could for a cracked evener and two broken tugs, and then we crawled together back to the stable. I unharnessed the horses, fed them some hay for consolation, gave a very watered-down report to my mother to pass on to my father when he came home from town with the grain he had gone to get ground, and then slunk off to the orchard to have a private service of Cursing the Harrow. Obviously, I had no future whatever as a farmer, probably not much of a future at all. I had no idea how my father would react to the disaster.

Dad stood on the porch and called me from my retreat. I came slowly to within earshot, dragging my chains.

"There's still time to finish that harrowing if you get right at it." He turned away.

I took a few steps nearer. "Want me to go back out there?"

"Yeah," over the shoulder.

"D'you see the harrow?"

"That it?" he said, pointing.

"Was," I said.

We focused exclusively on the task at hand. With a crowbar, maul, hammer, and plank, we reshaped the harrow, which was made of magnificently unbreakable spring steel; with binder twine and baling wire and a spare strap and some rivets we repaired the harness; we substituted a spare evener for the splintered one; and then he harnessed one horse while I harnessed the other. We were father and son again, farming again, repairing damage. Because no alternative presented itself, harrow and horses and I were soon heading back to the field of anxiety.

For the rest of the day I made very wide turns and, little by little, I slew the nemesis. And chopped it up. And harrowed it under.

Allis-Chalmers and the Holy Grail

By Justin Isherwood

Justin Isherwood is a potato farmer and writer, a combination of talents as rare as it is profound. Farming has been the Isherwood family's livelihood for six generations, with three generations tilling the soil and tapping maple trees in north-central Wisconsin.

Isherwood's writings on farm life blend his sense of humor with a keen eye for observing human nature. He has penned essays on farmers' addiction for sheds, an ode to overalls, a treatise on farm dogs, and an examination of what he believes was divine intervention in the invention of the first pickup truck.

His commentary has appeared in *Audubon*, *Harrowsmith*, *Country Life*, and the *Wall Street Journal* as well as on National Public Radio. His short pieces were collected into *Book of Plough: Essays on the Virtue of Farm, Family & the Rural Life.*

This excerpt on the battle between horse and tractor true believers comes from Isherwood's 1988 novel, *The Farm West of Mars*, which won the Wisconsin Idea Foundation literature award.

 I never drove horses; my dad did, as did his father and generations of fathers before. I wondered why I, of all those kin and links of farmers, was spared horses. I would have liked horses. My father loved horses, and at some turn of winter moon or mood did recount the glories of the time, though it was more an age than it was time alone, maybe even an epoch, when it was horse.

My Uncle Jim loved horses. He was my grandfather's brother who lived and farmed down the road, 160 rods exactly. There had been four brothers; Ed, Henry, George and Jim. Uncle Ed farmed on the Maine School Road, Henry cured houses of termites in St. Louis, Missouri. They had sisters but they got married off and belonged then to other families.

In my years, Uncle Jim was the only really old man available for inspection. Except maybe Mister Eckels, but I only saw him on Sunday when he was dressed up, and you can't tell anything real about a person on a Sunday morning. My own grandfather had died before he was old, I mean real real old. Died before I got a fix on what purpose age serves. Maybe if they had left him around to mildew I could have drawn some

1920s: Dawn of a New Age

Ma gives a winsome wave to Pa as he plows the family's forty acres in this oil painting by artist Walter Haskell Hinton. The war between farmers who believed in mechanical horsepower instead of flesh-and-blood horse power flared up with the advent of lightweight tractors. The Horse Association of America warned against the rise of farm tractors in its 1924 Annual Report, proclaiming "The horse and man made civilization: they should forever stand inseparable." Meanwhile, tractor visionaries such as Henry Ford took up the opposing side. Ford wrote in his 1926 autobiography, My Life and Work, *that "The farmer must either take up power or go out of business."*

conclusions, but they buried him straight off in the township cemetery. I touched his face when he was in a coffin in the bay window of the Boston Furniture Company and Funeral Parlor. They sold furniture in the front of the store and did funerals in the back. An overflow crowd was rewarded with the use of the stuffed sofas and chairs that were ever more comfortable than the wood folding chairs, meaning there were people who came late to funerals just so they could overflow into overstuffed. I knew my grandfather was dead 'cause he was hard. Told my brother Gary to touch him too 'cause I was a bit worried maybe death rubbed off. Like stone Grandfather was, if a little painted. I wondered, as a kid might, if the furniture of the Boston Funeral Parlor Company wasn't more than genuine leather.

Uncle Jim and my grandfather looked alike. They did not think alike; least not any time in the last fifty years. To my inspection George and Jim exercised the full range of hostile and antagonistic forces anywhere in the world. They acted civil enough on the outside, like at the Community Club, but by mutual agreement kept to opposing parties, their every opinion and method opposite. Whether on religion, the planting of rutabagas, white bread or whole wheat, tea, temperance, or horses; they were opposites.

Wasn't hate as much as horses. Jim loved horses like he loved the Republican Party, even in times when it was hard to love the Republican Party. On horses, Uncle Jim was absolute in his faith. Righteousness was measured by physical vigor, so any lack of moral superiority was readily apparent. At least it is apparent on farmers, for he who is up before first light and still afield at dusk is the rightful farmer, as measured by their earnestness. To a neutral observer this policy might seem nothing less than a desire to kill off the specimen by an overburden of physical zeal. But then neutral observers aren't righteous or else they won't be sitting there watching someone else work.

Since early in their careers as farmers, and next door neighbors, and brothers, it was obligatory what Jim and George had to say to each other was both righteous and vigorous, and about as extreme an utterance as it is possible to communicate. So it was necessary that everything they said to each other was at the extreme end of plausibility, never mind they were both Republicans, they so contrived their deeds and words as to end up on two different trees. This cruel crease

of dissimilarity ran the full length of the lives of George and Jim.

If George read in William Dempster Hoard's *Journal* that the silo method of corn preservation was a premium source of winter feed and happened to mention it aloud or to an intermediary, then Jim, within the week had proof and direct quote from the *Grange Journal* that silage is the cause of hard calving. The conflict of their passions extended to every mechanical object and philosophical treatise ever given the reality of words or cast iron. Should one take a position on any topic, tool, trend or touchstone, the other was obliged to assume the polar opposite.

Sometime just past the onset of the twentieth century, George offered a favorable opinion regarding internal combustion; Jim, though nearing that conclusion himself, had as a consequence to take the antithesis. That moral high ground being horses. For the next fifty years these two brothers of the town road as extended from the sandstone ledge of Bancroft to the state road twelve miles beyond, did wage the epic battle of horses versus tractors, and did so as if all human purpose and destiny depended on the outcome. Each side sent forth its propogandas, its slanders, had its spies, assigned its saints, gathered to its altar all the dear and holy objects and provisioned themselves for defense in case of sneak attack.

They argued over simple things: When to plant oats, whether it might by October freeze, they argued whether the winter just completed had been long, short, warm, cold, all the while it was the self-same winter. Each took, as statistics can demonstrate, a fair share of the prognostic victories. The only object on which they agreed was bib overalls; everything else was up for contest. Both recognized the purity and purpose of "overhauls," but vainly believed they had worn them before the other.

It is by natural consequence the farmer is a lean-loined creation. A fat farmer simply did not and could not exist, not if he was also righteous, meaning dawn to dusk righteous. The off-shoot of this was not lost on the manufacturers of bib overalls ... they didn't offer sizes. One size fit every farmer from the Ohio valley to the wheat flats of Saskatchewan. Never mind in the catalog three sizes were named: large, extra large and medium ... all were precisely the same cut. There was no small size. In fact what farmer who could lug forty sacks of white oats two stories in the hour be-

1900s: Proud tractor owners

"Just try to get your horse team to do this!" these confirmed tractor believers appear to be saying. While horses rarely tipped over, tractors too often did, so tractor makers hurried to promote the feats their machines were capable of in an effort to woo non-believers to their steam-powered steel horses. (Minnesota Historical Society)

tween milking and dark wanted to admit to a dry sneeze of a store clerk that he was small. Not on your life. The manufacturers of bibs knew what was forensically discernible about farmers. It did present a problem, since anatomy as expressed by mischievous DNA is a variable thing, meaning folks come in different sizes. Some got shoulders which is no problem because in bibs, shoulders don't count. Hams though were a problem. What bib overall makers did, and rather brilliantly, was to anticipate the design of the revival tent and establish this same format into a set of clothes. Simply by pulling the tent-stakes out a little is the overflow crowd accommodated. A large man undid some of the buttons, a small man cinched up a couple; fit

was accomplished in the same way as with the loincloth.

On a medium man the leg holes on a medium pair of bibs was exactly three times the circumference needed to fit the foot through. The result was a man could put his work shoes on first and not have to worry whether the shoe and sock fit through the pant leg, much less the galosh if not a snowshoe of the Alaskan design. The reverse was also true. The farmer could withdraw from his overhauls without first taking off his shoes. Bib overall makers did not ask what purpose farmers might put this innovation to; they didn't want to be responsible; they didn't want to be sued. If a man wanted to put his shoes on before his bibs, that

1937 Fordson N All-Around

Henry Ford was raised on a farm and he never forgot it. When Ford set out to change the world with his Model T automobile, he also had in the back of his mind a mechanical horse that would "lift the burden of farming from flesh and blood and place it on steel and motors," as he wrote in his autobiography. His Fordson tractor was unveiled in 1917, and by 1924 it was so ubiquitous that Ford exclaimed, "Over 75% of all tractors on American farms are Fordsons." Built in England, this All-Around version was Fordson's attempt to build a row-crop tractor for the North American market. Owners: Betty and Earl Resner of Grand Junction, Colorado. (Photograph by Ralph W. Sanders)

The Mule vs. the Fordson

By Charles Domeier of Pecatonica, Illinois

I grew up on a farm in Nebraska. Dad had always used mules until one day in about 1924, he came home with a new Fordson. It was harvest time, and Dad and I had been using two identical ground-driven binders pulled by excellent mule teams. Now Dad hooked the Fordson to one of the binders, which he drove, leaving me with the other and the team of mules. During that day, I and the mules passed Dad and the Fordson four times.

Needless to say, he was not too happy.

was his business. If he wanted to leave his shoes on but shuck his bibs in a hurry, that, too, was his business. Bibs were multi-faceted, multi-floral, multi-moral, and grossly over democratic, never mind Republicans wore them too. The manufacturers knew they were redesigning the heart and interior of civilized man as much as they were making clothes. They knew very well bibs on a person of medium format got in the way of his tying his shoes, this because it is still dark when he is tying his shoes. If he has to turn on the light to tie his shoes, it will wake the woman an hour early as could effect the matrimonial balance of agriculture, much less the western hemisphere, thus its success or failure, all because of the size of the leg holes in bib overalls. If a farmer can put on his shoes first, he might be inclined to start the fire in the stove before going to the barn. If he has to put on the bibs before the shoes and three days of junk in his pockets gets in the way of tying them at the fast try, the specimen is less inclined to catch the stove before morning chores. An early catch in the stove promoted harmony between the sexes, it raised the humor and the honor of the breakfast hour, it invigorated marriage, it underwrote Christianity. Bib overhauls, sized to fit a tied pair of shoes and attached barn rubbers through the leg holes, in the dark, a cold midwinter dark, knew this.

Uncle Jim was to remain devout to horses throughout his life and equally hate tractors for the same duration. Tractors, to Uncle Jim, were an abomination of human purpose and good sense. Horses were the true destiny as ordained by God, also Jehovah, Yahweh, Jesus Christ and St. Paul, and the perfect use of human and animal talent.

My father bought his first tractor in 1940, a used WC of the Allis-Chalmers Company. The price, two hundred and sixty dollars. The first trajectory my father offered at the world with his tractor was a casual deployment down the town road 160 rods, as went past Uncle Jim's house. He drove all the way across the marsh, crossing the eight plank bridges between our place and Bancroft village causing every one of them to rumble, which you can hear with both your ears stopped up 'cause the sound still comes through your feet. Uncle Jim heard it too. My dad drove the town road once in third gear for opulence, once in fourth gear for humiliation. He should not have done that because it was unChristian. That moment was to our

part of the township on par with the demonstration of the atom bomb at Hiroshima; it was way too demonstrative. For it was a declaration of technical superiority and that a propitious and unconditional surrender, by horses, would be accepted gracefully and with favorable terms. Uncle Jim saw it otherwise.

My grandfather's selection of tractors solidified all the doubts Uncle Jim had regarding tractors and similar machineries. He could see the terrible tattoo on George's face already, that reeking paralysis of character as is caused by tractors. Horses never set loose an overgrown hill of pride like that Julius Caesar posture George had the day he motored the town road on his Allis-Chalmers. Besides, what if the tractor stopped running somewhere between Bancroft and home, what then?

A horse, according to my Uncle Jim, is a solid thing. You don't have to know how a horse works any more than you have to understand biology to participate in it. And horses didn't involve the whole goddamn world. Horses came from mares and mares went with stallions and that is all it is necessary to know. Didn't have to know anything about spark gaps, bearing tolerances, shims, foot-pounds, gear-oil, spring tension or cold weather starting to get on with horses. If a farmer understood hay and oats and how not to water hot horses, then he understood enough. Where, Uncle Jim asked, where did tractors come from? Nobody really knows, do they? How do tractors work? Nobody knows that either. Uncle Jim was sure nobody knew. Uncle Jim understood horses; where they came from and exactly how. Had the when of the how marked on the calendar. What pasture to set the "how" loose in as the neighbor came over with the "when." Any fool can learn the way of horses, but engines? No sir, America was built by horses, fought over by horses. Did not all the Presidents of these colonies have horses? Or at the very least were horses asses? John Wesley's gospel was conveyed by horses, Ulysses Grant rode a horse, so did Mister Lee, so did Sherman . . . hell, God probably rode a horse. If rightfulness matters, it oughta stay at horse. With horses there is no danger of explosive fuels or engines flying apart to shuck a man's bean in a moment of mechanical wrath. A horse don't fly apart. Might stun you at new shoes but that's the whole of it. No sir, if there's God somewhere, whether in clouds, in the Bible, or in the muck of the Boney Vieux, he's a horse god. You wait and see, this tractor will ruin everything it touches and America too. Even in a bad year you can still tend horses. Where you at with tractors in a bad year? Buckled up and shackled to Pennsylvania tars? Uncle Jim knew Pennsylvania was halfway to hell already, in another hundred years could be all the way there. Besides, what comes of a man breathing tractor gasses all day? When a horse has the winds, what's left is still breathable. Don't warrant you try that with a tractor.

Uncle Jim was not fooled by progress. In his version only one sort of progress existed in the world and that was for a man and a woman with vows between them to advance. Everything else might be or might not be progress. Real progress was set up by getting chores done early, then supper, then blowing out the lights with the gloam still on. Which was as close as Uncle Jim came to public smut, and kids took honor in being allowed to hear Uncle Jim at close range when he lowered himself to preach on sex.

The Allis-Chalmers, even my father admitted, was pretty experimental, since he didn't have any machinery to mate with it. An improved tongue replaced the singletree of the horse-drawn mower to fit it on the tractor, same with the wagons. Soon after the binder was modified and the hay rake. Then Pa was in a fix, whether to turn hard to tractors or continue to straddle the middle position between the two domains. He took the path of Allis-Chalmers. Did it, he said, 'cause he didn't like beer drinkers at his threshing; my dad was a hard-thinking Methodist. With his own combine he didn't have to worry whether the whole fool crew got drunk the night before as to put his white oats at risk. The combine set forth my father's destiny. Soon after he bought a used wire-tie baler, Harry Precourt rode it and twisted the wire ends when he was supposed to, putting the clipped wire ends in a tin can out of fear for what hardware do to the insides of a cow.

The farm hung right there for awhile until my father could get his cant hook into wood and not just bark. That's when three sons followed after his first born daughter, provisioned was he with a sign from God to proceed straight on with tractors. In 1951 Pa bought another Allis-Chalmers, a Model WD, also a silo blower, an Allis-Chalmers corn chopper and round baler. Shortly after we all had our picture taken with the last horse to grace our farm.

When Dad bought that second tractor something in Uncle Jim broke, and his hope that tractors were a

passing fad. By 1951 the evidence suggested tractors were not another drifting miasma in the farm sector, Minneapolis-Moline, International Harvester, Ford, Ferguson, John Deere, J. I. Case, Oliver had their wares and promises out at every fair and cross-road feedmill. The long age of the horse was over, from Genghis Khan to Sitting Bull the horse people were done for. Uncle Jim knew it, saw it and with the refined vengeance of the vanquished, turned his back on the whole of it.

Meeting Uncle Jim on the town road came in the form of ritualized tragic opera. As a tractor approached, Uncle Jim pulled the team to the side of the road and stopped. Getting down from his rubber-tired freight wagon he walked around to the front of his team and stood with them waiting for the sinful monstrosity to pass. His back was turned. Uncle Jim was sure in his heart the tractor was evil. Steel axles, rubber tires, inner-tube, Timken bearings, those might be fair and worthy advances, but let civil-man be done with internal combustion. The petrol-engine had ruined the railroads, wiped the ocean clean of the China clippers and red-prowed Indiamen. The cause of it was that fool engine. Meet Uncle Jim on foot while hiking cows and he'd wave, pull his team over and talk away

the hour. At his garden he'd show off his red cabbage and a new strain of dahlia. But be aboard an engine and Uncle Jim ignored your presence, your existence, your very being, not once waving or calling out, instead his back turned, never to honor the tractor's passage. If three tractors of three neighbors were on the road all aimed for the hay fields, Uncle Jim waited them out. Sometimes he spent most of a forenoon traversing the 80 rods between his barn door and pasture gate. Waiting for the tractors to pass. Might take centuries, thousands, even millions of years, they would see it in the end how he was right; Uncle Jim could afford to wait. He knew he could wait out internal combustion, be it jet engine or the fusion reactor, he and horse in a distant time will be avenged. Horses would be back. Folks would learn sooner or later that tractors were not a good idea, much less righteous. Nature never intended them. Engines weren't honest. Horses shall return. Maybe horses are slow and some are given to wind, but a horse never had need for a lamp under its belly to start on a winter morning. Even if horses do hold back some if it's dark outside, what tractor can offer an opinion of hay weather? Good haying horse can smell a rain cloud far off as Kansas.

1910s: Tractor invasion

New tractors paraded out of factories across North America as the mechanical mule began to catch on with converts to the new philosophy of power farming. These gas-powered Universals rolled like an invading army down the main street of Stillwater, Minnesota, home of the prolific Universal Tractor Company and the Northwest Thresher Company. (Photograph by John Runk/Minnesota Historical Society)

In June all a farmer needs is a horse with a weather-nose and never again worry of moldy hay.

Good team of horses brings a man to twice as smart as nature made him. Meet a stranger on the road and a horse can tell if a man is a tramp, burn or hung out to dry. A horse can find its way home even when the driver can't, yes sir. All the way from the Keene Postal Station and Tavern . . . try that, smart boy, with your tractor. Look what tractors done to the world, never would have been world war if the earth were left to horses. Engines ruinated the world. Was war that spilled out the automobile. Uncle Jim was sure Wilson's war done it, done it to America, done it to him, done it to his horses. Democrats always start 'em. Don't mean to but they do just the same. War gives a boy a taste for liquor, fancy girls and hair oil; can't see himself as debonair out behind a horse.

When the world was horse a man could hear himself think. Tractors are all noise and spark, and pretty soon folks thinking they ain't smart if there isn't noisy upholstery on everything. Uncle Jim knew where it would end; right back at horses.

Uncle Jim died that September at ninety years and four. Died in the upstairs room of the farmhouse he built in 1907. Slept in the same room, same iron bed, same east windows for fifty years. Never once a night away from his home and iron bedstead. Died in his sleep. So stiff by morning it was difficult to get him down the narrow turn of the staircase, and his body set up. Had to stand his body on end to make the turn. Was like he made the stairs narrow on purpose so maybe they'd leave him there to desiccate in the east room, the one with the morning window and fifty years worth of dawn.

In October they sold his team of Belgians, who were grey and mellow beasts. They sold the red stallion from

1923 Bates Steel Mule

As most farmers thought in terms of a horse team for getting their farmwork done, it was only natural that the new tractor companies would capitalize on this reference and name their newfangled machines in honor of the beasts of burden they sought to replace. So, when the Bates Machine & Tractor Company of Joliet, Illinois, unleashed its crawler tractor in 1917, the name "Steel Mule" seemed ideal. Bates advertised its machine with the slogan, "This machine will do a hundred other things just like horses do them." Owner: Don D. Carman of Bennet, Nebraska. (Photograph by Ralph W. Sanders)

1945 Farmall BN

As the tractor won a place on the farm, many a horse suddenly found itself in retirement. Owner: Bill Wisnefske of Larsen, Wisconsin. (Photograph by Andy Kraushaar)

the woodlot, but the man had to shoot it to claim it. Nobody said it out loud, but Uncle Jim's absence from the township was awful and sudden. Dogs didn't have horseshit to roll in any more. We couldn't wait haying by watching for when Uncle Jim went out and the whole township knew haying was right 'cause Uncle Jim said it was right.

The hardest thing for farmers to quit when it came to tractors was the baptisms. A horse had a soul where the machine had a grease cup; accordingly horses had names and a few earned tombstones. They were friendly names: Dan, Prince, Andy . . . brawny names: Mephistopheles, Caesar, Permafrost . . . artful, sublime names: Cleopatra, Victoria, Cutty Sark . . . fragile names: Lilac, Daisy, Primrose. Joyous, meaningful, honest names. Names that took hold inside the beast and when you ask Mephistopheles to pull, he'd pull till his heart broke. All because of that sound uttered and in the mystery of devotion, pulled for all it was worth. No man alive, at least no farmer, could see that and not feel an earnest love for the great dumb beasts.

Tractors came from the factory with cryptic numbers, with curious combinations of alphabet: WC, the 30-20, the 12-20, the B, the Six, the GP. There was not

anything soulful about them and this failure stalled farming in a dark age longer than anything before or since. In due course tractors too got names; like horses they worked, they balked, they kicked, a few killed their keepers. Farmers came to name their tractors as carefully as they baptized their horses before. Nothing like Mephistopheles and Geronimo and Madam Bovary, but names never-the-less. There was an Alice, Roaring John, Moose-brains, Hot Spit, the Holy Inquisition. Nothing as majestic as horse names but names anyway. After all, tractors were only a generation deep into agriculture and besides, had Uncle Jim's curse on 'em.

Tractors were here to stay, least for awhile, till the curse found a better place to dig its toes in. Being my Uncle Jim's curse, sure as shellac it'd come in disguise. Tractors wouldn't up and melt or sprout weeds, instead suffer something more insidious, like a price on milk or #2 yellow corn that don't make sense. Or maybe a farmer moving his whole self to Florida and selling his land for a million dollars to people who each want a half acre, this when corn is worth half of nothing. Admittedly, not very likely. And not very soon, but if there is a thing Uncle Jim's curse has, it is patience.

Farewell Horses

By Orlan Skare of Willmar, Minnesota

My fascination with tractors and farm machinery started early, as a toddler and before my ability to recall. Mom told of a visit to Aunt Ida's in South Dakota where I found Uncle Emil's tractor and began to "crank" it with the front-hanging crank that early tractors had. Obviously I wasn't able to start it, and I came into the house, sputtering in Norwegian (my only language at that time) that I cranked and I cranked but it darn well didn't start!

While gasoline-powered tractors became increasingly common among neighboring farmers, it always seemed to me that Mom and Dad resisted this move, continuing to farm with horses. I could think of a dozen reasons to purchase a tractor, but there were always an equal number of reasons why "tractor farming" was a risky venture in our cashless economy. After all, horses consumed only home-grown oats and hay!

Each time another neighbor purchased a new tractor and sent their horses to the rendering works, I found our horses more distasteful. Aside from the fact that the implement operator had to view these draft horses from their broad posteriors, I remember them as being sweaty, smelly, and skitterish.

For a large animal, a horse can be frightened by the most insignificant incident. A loud noise, or an unfamiliar movement however small, can send a team of hulking horses on a runaway, at best causing damage to the towed machinery. Serious farm accidents and deaths were often due to an operator unable to jump clear of the bouncing machine.

Our first move toward a tractor was the purchase of a "bug," which consisted of a Ford truck chassis, shortened, with the cab removed, and fitted with a drawbar and a hay bucket. This was a fairly efficient tractor for bringing hay to the overshot stacker, but was less efficient as drawbar power for tillage machines.

World War II with the rationing of farm machinery and the total unavailability of rubber-mounted tractors delayed our final conversion to tractor farming until 1947.

Because I soon went away to college, Dad and young brother Elmo were the major beneficiaries of this move. However I did operate this tractor, a Ford Model 8N, some and loved it. The fascination with tractors probably helped me decide to join International Harvester following my graduation from college.

But even the horse-drawn implements held a certain fascination for me. More complex implements like hay mowers and grain binders were mechanical marvels, employing speed reduction gears, the converting of rotating motion to oscillating motion, automatic twine tying knotters, and almost every mechanical principle known in the Thirties.

A machine as complicated as a grain binder required good maintenance and fine-tuning to keep it operating smoothly. Dad, a good farm mechanic, sometimes allowed me to help him. I mastered enough complex engineering technology so that in my own parenting years I could assemble my young daughter's tricycle—with a little help from her.

There was much that was pleasant about operating a horse-drawn implement. Horses are not very noisy, and the sounds are limited to those of the implement at work. The moldboard of a plow carefully turns a 14-inch strip of stubble into a continuous black ribbon extending the length of the field. The sickle bar of a hay mower carefully lays a swath of standing alfalfa unto the ground where it can cure to become a nutritious winter feed for dairy cows. Even the less appealing manure spreader lays a band of organic fertilizer that helps stimulate the renewal of next year's growth.

My fascination with farm machinery continues today. Agricultural technology has changed greatly in size, in the utilization of electronics, and in operator comfort. Air conditioned cabs, cushioned seats, and advanced hydraulics make operation less physically tiring. Yet a trip to one of the late-summer outstate threshing shows is for me a pleasant transport back to the 1930s.

Chapter 2

Home-Brewed Mechanical Mules

"Don't let your old Ford or Chevrolet go to waste. Use it to make a practical general-purpose tractor that has the pulling power of from two to four horses, yet costs less the price of one horse. Simply remove the body of your Ford Model 'T' or 'A,' or a 1926 to 1931 Chevrolet, and attach the Sears Thrifty Farmer Tractor Unit—a quick, easy operation."
—Sears Roebuck catalog, 1939

When faced by the pricetag of a new Fordson tractor in the 1920s, many farmers looked instead at their old, broken-down Ford Model T automobile with renewed fondness. They gathered up their welding torches, some scrap metal, and set to work, transforming the skeleton of that ancient Tin Lizzy into a brand-new, home-brewed mechanical mule.

Often these homemade farm tractors served their ingenious makers for years, if not decades. Some homegrown tractors were mere stopgap vehicles used until the farmer could afford a Farmall. Others were well-engineered machines that rose above the sum of their disparate parts to become legends in their farm communities, bestowing renown on the farmer who eschewed the factory-built variety of tractor.

1920s: Doodlebug
Main photo: *Homemade tractors were often affectionately known as "doodlebugs," "thunderbugs," or a variety of other endearing and invariably cute names. When the collection of mismatched parts didn't want to start on a cold morning or failed in a field far from the homeplace, farmers had a full vocabulary of other, less affectionate names for them as well. (Photograph by J. C. Allen & Son)*

1910s: Tractor kit advertisement
Inset: *Numerous do-it-yourself kits to convert automobiles into tractors were offered in newspapers and magazines throughout North America in the 1910s and 1920s.*

$125 00
F.O.B. DETROIT
FITS ANY FORD

"The TRACTOR UNIVERSAL"

The New **TRACFORD**

—anticipates a nation-wide demand

The TRACFORD is the tractor sensation of the year—the development long awaited by agricultural America.

Sturdy—thoroughly tested—proven for every farm use—fits the standard Ford car—works only on high gear—has a 9 to 1 gear reduction—DOES NOT OVERHEAT—simple—dependable —none other like it.

It is "the tractor universal."

Tractor and Implement Dealers!

Here is the chance for you.

TRACFORD demand is limited only by the number of Fords owned by farmers in your county. Every one a prospect. And a live one! All have been waiting for something—something you can show them in the TRACFORD. Its appearance will interest and its performance will sell it.

All the objections you have heard about the big tractor—initial cost—excessive weight— fuel consumption—mechanical troubles—are overcome in the TRACFORD. It multiplies Ford power and utilizes Ford efficiency.

Dealers are being signed up daily—large areas of choice territory are already gone. And immediate deliveries of demonstrators are being made.

Also, we are preparing an extensive campaign of farm paper advertising to help YOU. It will be nation-wide in scope. Get in on this before your county is taken by a competitor.

Write today for full description of our proposition.

Send for "The Tracford Catechism." It answers the questions you want to ask.

THE STANDARD-DETROIT TRACTOR CO.
1506 Fort Street West
DETROIT, MICHIGAN

Iron

By Bruce Bair

Entitled *Good Land, or, My Life as a Farm Boy*, Bruce Bair's memoir of growing up on his family's wheat farm near Goodland, Kansas, reads like a homegrown version of William Shakespeare's *King Lear*. The farm is the kingdom of Bair's father, Harold, a strong, stern, stubborn man who farmed with an inner fury as if he was waging war with fate.

Bair's memoir is not a romantic look book at the farm life, but by simply writing of the good and bad times on the farm, he exorcises demons and at the same time waxes nostalgic. Bair left the family farm to pursue a career as a writer and has worked on newspapers from Montana to South Dakota and back to his native Kansas. As he himself admits, there is something intangible that continually draws him back to the farm.

This chapter from *Good Land* tells of his father's genius with metal and an acetylene torch. It was a skill necessary for survival on a pioneer farm, a skill that gave birth to many home-brewed farm tractors.

 The Kansas farmer, often an immigrant from the old country, brought with him woodworking and stone-hewing skills. He was a carver and a craftsman. He could cure and tan leathers or tongue-and-groove rough-sawed lumber to make a stock tank. But the Plains were farmed with iron. Even the rheumy-eyed old-timers at the Bird City Threshing Bee have forgotten those old-world crafts. Instead they restore twenties' and thirties' one-cylinder engines or apply green paint to old John Deeres. Plainsmen are metal workers, mechanics, and good shots.

Iron makes tools that wear out slowly and stay sharp and without it the Plains would still be grassland. As you ramble about on old farmsteads, among the fist-sized chunks of foundation rock and finger-sized pieces of crockery scattered by iron implements, a rusted piece of scrap iron pulled from the dirt turns out to be a steel step from a wooden wagon. The wood is long gone, rotted, burned in a stove. With a little brushing off, the buggy step could be bolted to wood and would still be strong enough to support a man.

Steel makes our pistons and gears and plowshares and the frameworks of our machines, but as strong as it is, it constantly breaks or bends and must be mended or returned to shape again. Every farmer is a steel worker and a man who can bend iron never runs entirely out of confidence.

My father stands in the dim shop with the acetylene torch in his hand, adjusting the red knob which controls the acetylene and the green knob which allows the oxygen to flow. When he operates the striker, flint on steel, the torch ignites with a small flaring ex-

1910s: Do-it-yourself tractor

Henry Ford's Model T had proven itself the farmer's friend, providing cheap and cheerful transportation. With the rise of power farming, many farmers now converted their tin lizzies into tractors, often with the aid of a kit such as Standard-Detroit Tractor Company's Tracford. If you wrote for "The Tracford Catechism" brochure, you too were sure to become a convert.

plosion. This is on our first farm, the one I grew up on. The shop is tin-sided, with high concrete footings and dusty windows over the shop bench on the west side. It is a multipurpose building, joined on the east to a boxcar which serves as a storage room for sacks of feed. The boxcar was lifted on its foundation three feet above the floor before the shop was added on. Inside the shop, a wide concrete lip runs along the front of the boxcar so sacks can be more easily loaded and unloaded from wagons. Below the boxcar is a pit running its length, exuding smells of rotten grain and ancient grease and festooned with the webs and egg sacks of black widow spiders. It is a fearsome hole which I might, in my bravest moments, peer into from the bottom step, but which my father forages in without fear, plunging his hand into dust and webs and crevices amid junk to drag forth what to anyone else would be a forgotten piece of iron.

Harold is obsessed. A thin milo crop needs grinding into ensilage, but the big Bearcat cutter he bought the year before barely strains under its two-row load. It's too slow, so he means to make things more efficient. What he is doing is welding an old McCormick binder to the Bearcat and devising a feeding mechanism so that the feed cut by the binder will pour like a waterfall into the throat of the cutter. The binder cuts six rows at a time, tripling the feeding capacity. He uses the acetylene torch to cut the steel required and the electric welder to put it back together.

He wants me to hold things. I am a portable locking pliers. He gets mad when the sparks fly on me and burn me and I let go. He tells me to get out when he arc welds. The arc is so bright it casts flickering shadows like lightning against the shop walls. If you stare at it long enough you'll burn your eyes. But it is almost impossible not to look in fascination at the tiny blue sun.

He wants a nine-sixteenths, but I can never find them fast enough. When I ask where they are, he always says "over there" or "look on third shelf," when third shelves loom everywhere. I'm proud when I find it.

"About time," he grumps. He's already used the pliers he carries in the pocket of his overalls to wrench the rusted nut free. At school, we have bragging contests about how strong our fathers are.

"My Dad is as strong as a telephone pole."

"My Dad is stronger than a horse."

"My Dad," I say, "is stronger than steel," which ends all argument.

The miscegenation of the binder and the Bearcat gives my father trouble. At supper he complains. "I can't get the feed right."

In his chair, he wrestles with the problem, making gears of his hands and chains of his arms and turning them with his mind. By morning, he has the problem worked out and the sparks fly. He thinks he is a genius when he tows the contraption to the field and it works for a while.

"Now, that's a feed cutter," he says.

It's more complex than that. He's been to Garden City, where a farmer with a welder manufactures low slung green trailers from sheet metal and airplane tires. He bought one. The trailer has a little trough where the rear wheels of the ensilage truck are supposed to rest, so it can be dragged backwards through the field behind the ensilage cutter. This eliminates the truck driver.

Other farmers slow down when they see this incredible complex of machinery being dragged through the field behind the John Deere R. I think some of them will go home and laugh so hard they won't be able to digest their mashed potatoes. A 1930s vintage binder attached to a 1950s Bearcat, with a 1942 R.E.O. truck dragged behind on B-29 tires. "You ought to of seen it."

But it worked, at least for a while, though it always broke down because the hitch wasn't quite right or the feed mechanism Harold had built from scratch wasn't strong enough, but mostly because God had stupid ideas with hard labor.

Stubbornly, he kept at it another year. Now, thirty years later, if you want to look, you can still find the trailer, the Bearcat and the binder in the kochia weed-covered junk pile, although considerable chunks of metal have been sliced off them for other projects.

With enough stock steel, a torch and an electric welder, you can build anything.

1914 Geneva Adapto-Tractor

Above: *"Do 2 days work in 1" promised an advertisement for the Adapto-Tractor from the Geneva Tractor Company of Geneva, Ohio. Numerous small-time entrepreneurs advertised their kits for converting Ford Model T automobiles into tractors in tiny line ads in the back pages of farming newspapers and magazines throughout North America. The Adapto-Tractor replaced the rear end of the tin lizzy with special gearing and cleated steel wheels to aid it in pulling a plow. Owner: Glenn Heim of Lockport, Illinois. (Photograph by Randy Leffingwell)*

1920s: Build-your-own-tractor plans

Left: *These plans from a 1920s magazine instructed those handy with a wrench on how to build their own tractor from old car parts. No machining skills were required.*

1920s: Ma, Pa, and home-brewed tractor

Overleaf: *Ma and Pa donned their Sunday best to stand proudly for a portrait with their homemade iron horse. (Glenbow Archives)*

Homemade Tractor

By Jerry Apps

Jerry Apps is one of Wisconsin's finest folk historians. He grew up on a farm in the Chain O' Lakes region of Wisconsin, a background that has inspired his writing and his numerous books, including *Barns of Wisconsin, Rural Wisdom: Time-Honored Values of the Midwest, Cheese: The Making of a Wisconsin Tradition, Breweries of Wisconsin*, and *One-Room Country Schoolhouse: History and Recollections from Wisconsin*.

The closest book to his heart may be his collection of childhood reminiscences entitled *When Chores Were Done: Boyhood Stories*, which chronicles his farm youth. His writing is sentimental yet also realistic in describing both the joys and the hardships of life on the farm.

This chapter from *When Chores Were Done* tells of a neighborhood genius who built a farm tractor with his bare hands using the remains of old trucks, spare parts cannibalized from other machinery, and his own down-home know-how.

FARMFORD Pa had a letter from the County Agricultural Agent saying he was eligible to buy a new tractor but there just weren't any because of the war. The demand was too great, and the number of tractors too small.

One day Pa stopped at Jim Colligan's shop in Wild Rose. Colligan was a welder-blacksmith, a kind of jack-of-all-trades who repaired farm equipment, sharpened plow points, and welded things together. Colligan wasn't a big man, not as tall as Pa, but he had the broadest shoulders I'd ever seen and the thickest arms. He was an inventor of sorts, cobbling together old things to make new things. Pa and Jim had been friends for many years—they had known each other since they were kids. They talked about the shortage of farm tractors.

"Been thinking about making a tractor," Jim said.

"How might you do that?" Pa asked.

"Well," Jim said. "Chet Hansel just bought himself a new truck and his old Model A Ford truck is still in pretty good shape. I was thinking of making a tractor out of it."

And that's what he did. He shortened the truck's frame. In place of regular truck tires, he acquired a pair of huge old tires that the county discarded from one of its snowplows. Colligan bolted these tires to the truck wheels and left them flat, to provide more traction for the tractor. With some sheet metal, he fashioned a hood to cover the engine, and he made a seat for the operator to sit on. He covered the whole thing with aluminum paint and drove it out to the farm one summer day in 1942.

What a beauty. I was eight years old and knew I was surely not old enough to drive this fine machine. But right then I looked forward to riding on it, along with my father.

1929 Thieman

The idea was simple and brilliant: The Thieman Harvester Company of Albert City, Iowa, rounded up scrap automobiles—Ford Model As, Chevrolets, and Dodge Fours—and salvaged usable components to be rebuilt into the ultimate economy tractor. A sales hit during the Great Depression years, the Thieman retailed for a mere $185—you just supplied your own engine and bolted it into the frame, and you had a fine iron workhorse. This 1929 Thieman was powered by a Ford Model A motor. Owner: Palmer Fossum of Northfield, Minnesota. (Photograph by Randy Leffingwell)

Pa climbed on and made a couple of spins around the farmyard grinning like a Cheshire cat that had just caught a bumblebee. This was the first time he'd ever owned a tractor. Ever. He never showed much emotion, but this day it was obvious that he looked forward to sitting on this tractor and plowing, cutting grain, disking, and dragging. The tractor would make these tasks much easier compared to driving horses. Since he was a young lad, he had followed behind a team, usually walking as the team pulled a plow, a disk, or a drag. Now he could ride, and he would be ahead of the dust for a change, rather than walking in it. This was particularly true when working with a sixteen-foot-wide drag used to smooth ground before planting. The drag teeth, only three or four inches long, stirred up a considerable dust, particularly if the soil happened to be a little dry. Our sandy farm was usually dry, so dust was a part of many farm operations.

Though the tractor was truly wonderful and would soon have a great influence on how we farmed, it had its faults. The mechanical brakes were not good. It took great strength to push the brake pedal enough to engage them, particularly if the tractor happened to be on a rather steep hill. The tractor's transmission was, of course, a truck's transmission. Tractors must move only two or three miles per hour when doing heavy jobs like plowing, pulling rocks, or disking. The transmission had four speeds. Dual low, low, second, and high. Only dual low was slow enough and powerful enough for farm work. In high gear, the former truck reached speeds of forty-five or fifty miles an hour. With the larger than normal tires on the back, the machine moved even faster. Pa laid down the law early. "Whoever drives this tractor will never, ever, put it in high gear. You'll kill yourself and probably somebody else." At the moment, he was talking to himself since he was the only person on the farm who knew how to drive this new invention.

Second gear was also too fast for farm work, but might occasionally be used to drive to and from the fields, if the person was careful. Low was too fast for any heavy farm work, but could be used for such light jobs as toting an empty wagon or maybe pulling a drag. Early in the fall, Pa hooked the tractor to his new David Bradley double-bottomed plow. It plowed two twelve-inch furrows at a time. The tractor's four-cylinder engine putted as ribbons of freshly turned soil stretched across the twenty-acre field.

"Works like a charm," Pa said that night when he drove the shiny silver tractor into the shed and pulled shut the doors. "Cuts through alfalfa sod like butter."

Frank and Charlie, our draft horses that ordinarily pulled the plow, grazed quietly in the corner of the barnyard. They were growing fat and soft from lack of work.

That October, when we began digging potatoes, Pa said it was my turn to learn how to drive the tractor. Chain O' Lake School dismissed for two weeks of potato vacation so all the kids could help with the potato harvest. Some schools in the state had a spring vacation. Not Chain O' Lake. We had potato vacation in the fall when every man, boy, woman, and girl helped with the harvest so we could finish before the first killing frost ruined the crop.

Pa dropped the draw pin through the tongue of the steel-wheeled wagon, hooking it firmly to the tractor. Earlier he'd sawed several feet off the tongue because hooked to a tractor the tongue could be much shorter than when he used the team. He piled the wagon high with empty one-bushel wooden potato crates, and we drove out to the potato field. Pa hired Weston Coombes to help fork the potatoes out of the ground, and Weston and I sat on the wagon, our feet dangling over the side and kicking into the dirt when we wanted to.

My job was to pick up potatoes that Pa and Weston dug. They marched backwards, side by side across the field, each digging two rows of potatoes with six-tine barn forks. I followed along with a five-gallon pail, picking up the potatoes and dumping my full pail into one of the wooden boxes that we'd strung out across the twenty-acre field.

I still hadn't driven the tractor and wondered what Pa meant when he said today was the day I would learn. As noon approached, Pa stopped digging and suggested we load the filled boxes and haul them to the potato cellar near the chicken house.

"Come with me," Pa beckoned, as we walked to the homemade tractor parked under an oak tree that had turned a beautiful shade of reddish-brown. He hopped on the seat, pulled on the choke wire, pushed the starter button, and the engine caught the first time. Then he slid to the ground.

"Here," he said. "You drive. You're old enough to steer this thing while we pick up potato boxes."

"But how do I start moving?"

1920s: Homemade tractor and cultivator

Rube Goldberg himself would have been dazzled by the ingenuity required to craft this home-brewed tractor-cultivator unit. Built largely from two-by-four boards and miles of drivebelts and chains, this intricate machine was an incredible example of creativity and pioneer spirit. (Photograph by J. C. Allen & Son)

"Just push in the clutch, slip the shifting lever into dual low, put your other foot on the gas pedal, slowly let out the clutch, and push a little on the gas at the same time."

Sounded easy enough. I pushed in the clutch. I'd done this many times before, when I was play driving, so I knew how. I pulled on the lever and shifted into dual low. This I had also practiced before. Now I pushed on the gas pedal, and the engine roared a little and the machine began to vibrate. I pushed on the gas pedal some more.

"Not too much gas," Pa cautioned. He stood just back of me, on the tongue of the wagon. Slowly I let out the clutch, momentarily forgetting that my other foot continued to push on the gas pedal. With a mighty lurch, the tractor jumped forward, nearly tossing my father off his perch.

"Take your foot off the gas! Take your foot off the gas!" he yelled. I eased up on the gas pedal, and we moved slowly along the field. I was driving. By myself. For real. When we got to the end of the field, Pa showed me how to make a wide turn with the wagon, so the tractor's big rear tires wouldn't run into the front wheel of the wagon and break the wooden tongue. This I did without incident. I pushed in the clutch, shifted the lever into neutral, and jumped off the seat. A big smile spread across my face, and I felt a great sense of accomplishment. I heard people talking about feeling like a man. This was surely what it was like. Being a man was a fine feeling.

"You're not done yet," Pa said. "Drive back across the field while Weston and I load these potato boxes on the wagon. Stop when I tell you to."

This time I did better with the clutch and gas pedal,

and the tractor began moving along the soft potato ground. I stopped by the first several potato boxes while Weston and Pa promptly loaded them onto the wagon. Then I drove on. It was going well, exceedingly well. What was so complicated about driving a tractor, I wondered? Why all the fuss? There was nothing to it. A little steering to avoid running over the potato boxes and the potato plants not yet dug, a little thinking about how to let out the clutch and push down on the gas pedal at the same time, and listening to Pa say when I should stop and start. After two or three stops and starts, I had it down pat. I sat up straight on the tractor seat, hoping someone like maybe Jim Kolka would pass by on the road and see me driving the tractor. Kolkas didn't have a tractor—not a homemade one, not a factory-made one. Nothing. They depended for all their pulling on a pair of buckskin-colored draft horses, a rather tired pair that plodded along in a truly unspectacular way. What a great thing it would be if Jim or one of the other neighbor kids saw me driving this shiny new tractor, even if it wasn't factory built and didn't have the name John Deere or McCormick Deering or Fordson stamped on it. Model A Ford was good enough for me. Besides, everybody knew what a Model A Ford was. Several neighbors had Model A Ford cars and they swore by them, at them sometimes too, when they wouldn't start.

1923 Shaw Tractorized Car

Facing page, top: *The Shaw Manufacturing Company of Galesburg, Kansas, offered a conversion kit for both the Ford Model T and Model A and Chevrolet cars that turned tin lizzies into what looked like hot-rodded tractors. Following the directions, farmers junked their Fords' cabs and most amenities, bolted on Shaw's driveline and oversized wheels, and set out to plow the back forty. When all the parts were bolted together, the Shaw—and machines like it—became the ultimate budget Fordson. Owner: Fred Heidrick of Woodland, California. (Photograph by Randy Leffingwell)*

1928 Fordson Trackson

Facing page, bottom: *As if kits to convert Ford automobiles into tractors weren't enough, other companies offered kits to convert tractors into better tractors. Many of these kits were focused on the ubiquitous and supremely adaptable Fordson, such as this crawler conversion kit from the Trackson Company of Milwaukee, Wisconsin. In fact, Trackson's engineering was so good, the Caterpillar Company of Peoria, Illinois, bought the firm in 1951. Owner: Richard Stout of Washington, Iowa. (Photograph by Ralph W. Sanders)*

I approached the top of a rather steep hill. I stopped while Pa and Weston lifted several more potato boxes on the wagon, then I eased ahead, not quite sure how I should stop mid-hill. Stop I surely must for four or five filled potato boxes sat waiting half-way down the slope. Slowly I eased forward, the tractor gears holding the load back and making driving easier.

"Whoa!" Pa yelled. Much later, when we no longer had horses on the farm, he still yelled "Whoa!" when he meant stop.

I confidently pushed in the clutch and, rather than stop, the tractor began gaining speed.

"Push on the brake!" Pa yelled. I'd practiced this earlier but when the tractor was standing still. I pushed as hard as I could but nothing happened. The tractor with the partially loaded wagon of filled potato boxes moved even faster.

"Push on the brake!" Pa yelled again with some concern in his voice. I began staring at the brake pedal and my foot that somehow wasn't accomplishing the right thing. Glancing down was a major mistake.

"Look out for the potato boxes!" Pa yelled.

I looked up to see the right front tractor wheel hit the first wooden box dead center. I heard a sickening, splintering sound as the wood broke. I saw potatoes rolling down the hill. Then, before I could recover, I hit the next box, and the next, and the next, and somehow missed the last one on the hillside. At the bottom of the hill, I let out the clutch and killed the engine. I put my hands over my face, expecting the worst, when Pa caught up with the runaway rig.

"You hurt?" he asked, out of breath.

"Nah," I answered. "Smashed some boxes, didn't I?" The obvious was all I could think to say.

"Yup. Hop down and help Weston and me pick up the spilled potatoes and the kindling wood."

That's all he said. No punishment. No tongue lashing. Later, he showed me how to brace myself on the seat so I could get more leverage out of my right leg and push the brake far enough to stop the tractor. He also reminded me that had I gently let out the clutch, the tractor would also have stopped.

As I think about it now, I learned a lot more than a valuable driving lesson that day. I learned I shouldn't become confident too quickly when doing something new like driving a tractor. And I gained a new respect for Pa, too. By the end of the potato season, I was driving our shiny new tractor everywhere.

Chapter 3

Milestone Tractors

"I have not heard many farmers rhapsodize about machines, except perhaps for ones they used during childhood—two-cylinder Deere tractors or one of the early Farmalls."
—Verlyn Klinkenborg, *Making Hay*

In the long history of farm tractors, there have been horrible failures, mediocre machines, and those tractors that you could not pay a farmer enough to buy off his hands.

Some milestone tractors represented great revolutions in technology, such as the arrival of the three-point hitch on the Ford-Ferguson 9N. Others represented an evolution in quality, such as John Deere's Models A and B. And still others, such as International Harvester's Farmall, won the respect of farmers everywhere for their all-around capabilities.

1920s: Milestone tractor
Main photo: *Few tractors—in fact, few* machines *in general—proved as revolutionary as the well-named Farmall from the International Harvester Company of Chicago, Illinois. When it made its inauspicious debut in 1924, its all-purpose, row-crop design became a watershed for farm tractor engineering. This farmer doesn't look like he'd be willing to part with his Farmall no matter the price. (Photograph by J. C. Allen & Son)*

1950s: Oliver calendar
Inset: *Oliver celebrated its milestone Model 77 tractor in the pin-up pages of the firm's 1950 calendar.*

Caterpillar Hall of Fame

By Bob Feller

To baseball fans—and Caterpillar collectors—Bob Feller needs no introduction. Born and raised on a farm in Van Meter, Iowa, Feller stepped up to the pitching mound for the Cleveland Indians when he was a mere seventeen years old to throw what would quickly become a legendary fastball. After eighteen years with the Indians, Feller retired from baseball in 1956. Just six years later, he was elected to the Baseball Hall of Fame.

Feller has traveled the United States throwing baseballs, served in the U.S. Navy in the Pacific, and seen the bright lights of the big city. But you can't take the Iowa farm boy out of the man, and after his retirement from playing ball, Feller began to look back with a sense of nostalgia to the tractor he drove as a youth on his family's Iowa farm. That sentimentality inspired him to buy his first vintage Caterpillar, which led to purchasing a second one and eventually a whole fleet of old crawler iron.

 When my father bought the first Caterpillar tractor in Iowa in the early 1930s to use on our family farm, everybody said he was crazy. "It won't work," folks told him. People in our part of the country drove Fordsons or Farmalls, Johnny Poppers or Olivers—tractors with wheels on them. Nobody used a Caterpillar with those crazy crawler treads on them. It simply wasn't *right*.

Well, naturally they were all wrong. That Cat Twenty proved itself on our farm and made a convert of me and many another farmer.

Our family's farm was located in the countryside near Van Meter in the south-central part of the state. Working our land, I put in many hours at the controls of that Cat Twenty, as well as the twelve-foot Caterpillar combine that my dad purchased to run with it. They were solid machines that served us well for many years. My fascination with Caterpillars grew from those roots and continues to grow today.

I left the family farm to earn my living throwing baseballs. When I was seventeen years old in 1936, I made my major league debut pitching for the Cleveland Indians against the St. Louis Cardinals. Over the years, I dueled from the pitching mound with some of the all-time greats, batters such as Ted Williams and Joe DiMaggio—just me against them. Some of the veterans of those days said I threw the fastest pitches they had ever seen.

We all took time out from baseball during the World War II years; I served with the U.S. Navy aboard

1930s Caterpillar R2

The R2 5E crawler was built between 1934 and 1937, based on specifications drafted by the U.S. military. This rare R2 had been owned since new by the U.S. Navy. Owner Larry Maasdam obtained it from a salvage yard in Fairfield, California. The R2 was in good condition when he found it, needing only new paint. (Photograph by Andrew Morland)

the USS Alabama from December 1941 to August 1945. I returned to the mound in 1945 and remained true to the Cleveland Indians until my retirement from baseball in 1956. At the end of eighteen years of throwing fastballs for the Indians, I had a record of 266 wins against 162 losses, a lifetime ERA of 3.25, and 2,581 strikeouts. In 1962, I was elected to the Baseball Hall of Fame.

But despite my achievements on the baseball fields, part of my heart still belonged to the farm fields of my youth. Nostalgia for hallmarks of our roots seems to hit us harder as we grow older. For me, as for many farmers, one of the ties to my youth was the Caterpillar Twenty that I operated as a kid in the 1930s. I decided I wanted to track down another Twenty, which I soon did. Little did I know, but my life as a Cat collector had begun.

Since finding the Twenty, my small Caterpillar collection continues to grow. It's kind of my own personal Caterpillar "hall of fame" that includes my favorite Cat models: the Twenty, two Tens, a Forty, Twenty-Two, Twenty-Five, Twenty-Eight, and a D4. Someday soon I hope to add to the collection.

You can look at the latest Caterpillar today and see the history in the machine. The lineage of the Holt and Best machines, the steam age, the perfection of the crawler system, the early gas tractors, and Cat's industry-leading development of diesel power are all in a modern Cat. And that's part of what makes the Caterpillar story so great.

Another aspect of Caterpillar's greatness is that the machines are so versatile, a fact that is shown in the roster of Cat collectors. We come from all walks of life. Some come from a farming background. Other people's fascination with Cats started from working with them on construction sites, logging crews, road-grading jobs—anything and everything a Caterpillar can do.

1929 Caterpillar Twenty
Baseball Hall of Famer Bob Feller sits at the controls of his Caterpillar Twenty. Feller was a farm boy from Van Meter, Iowa, who grew up piloting a similar Twenty before he went off to earn his fame throwing fastballs for the Cleveland Indians. After retiring from baseball, nostalgia for his childhood on the farm renewed his interest in Cats. Today, this Twenty is just one of the Caterpillar crawlers in his collection. (Photograph by Ralph W. Sanders)

Old Tractors Still Going Strong

By Frank Lessiter

Frank Lessiter is a rural renaissance man. He is a farmer, a book publisher, and an author. He worked his family's centennial farm, which was founded in 1853, near Lake Orion, Michigan. He also runs Lessiter Publications, which publishes and sells a wide variety of technical books related to all aspects of agriculture.

Last but not least, Frank is the author of *Centennial Farm: How Six Generations Farmed the Land*, which chronicles his family's farming history. The book is like a family scrapbook, chock full of photographs and recollections from three generations of the Lessiter family.

This selection tells of the family's faithful tractors, a series of different Fordsons, Fords, and International Harvester Farmalls. While the tractors may have been different colors on other farms, the respect for and the fond memories of the "mechanical mule" were often the same.

Having been a teenager at Lohill Farm in the early 1950s, I fondly remember the slick new Ford Jubilee and Farmall Super H tractors coming off the delivery trucks.

I don't remember all of the economic details, but 1953 and 1954 must have been extremely good farming years for us because we bought new tractors both years. In 1954, the decision was made to switch to baling hay, and this meant buying the Farmall Super H and a PTO-powered International baler.

Both tractors are still going strong today at my sister and brother-in-law's farm west of Lapeer, Michigan. As you might guess, both tractors would bring more dollars today than Dad paid for them forty-five years ago!

Besides a couple teams of Belgian horses, Dad and Grandpa Frank had farmed with several older Ford and Fordson tractors. In fact, the Lessiter family's relationship with the company goes back to 1902 when Henry Ford visited the farm to examine a Shorthorn bull as a potential herd sire for his herd. That was a year before the Ford Motor Company was officially formed and four years before ex-farm boy Henry Ford started thinking about producing tractors.

By 1917, Ford was building the Fordson Model F tractor in Ireland. It had an 18-horsepower, four-cylinder engine and featured a three-speed, worm-reduction gear system. In 1918, 6,000 of these tractors were built at a Detroit factory. Within a few years, Ford grabbed 70 percent of the world's tractor market and produced 101,898 tractors in 1923. The 1922 Fordson sold for only $395!

When the 1953 Ford Jubilee tractor was introduced to celebrate the fiftieth anniversary of the Ford Motor

1920s: Old-timer still going strong

A veteran of many hours behind the wheel of a tractor, this farmer pauses in his chores atop his favored Case. (Photograph by J. C. Allen & Son)

Company, Dad was among the early buyers.

Larger and heavier than the 8N tractor it replaced, the Jubilee had an overhead-valve, four-cylinder, 134-cubic-inch engine. Completely restyled, it no longer resembled the popular 8N Ford tractor or the Ferguson TO-30, a major competitor which came out in 1951.

What I remember most about this tractor was the "Golden Jubilee Model 1903-1953" nose medallion used to promote the founding of the company in 1903. This medallion was made only during the fiftieth anniversary year; there was a revised star-encircled medallion on the 1954 tractors—about the only change made in that year s production.

A non-live PTO was standard on the Jubilee tractor and a live PTO was optional. The brakes were improved and a better governor was built. The muffler was moved from under the engine to under the hood to reduce the chance for a hot muffler causing fires in dry straw. The tractor also featured a Ford-designed, camshaft-driven pump mounted on the engine.

These Jubilee tractors were painted red and gray, an exciting change from the gray Fordson and Ford tractors seen for years. So much for the auto philosophy of Henry Ford Sr., whose credo was, "Any color as long as it's black."

It was more than just coincidence that a new Ford tractor made its debut during the fiftieth anniversary year of the company. To fully understand the situation, you need a little history.

The revolutionary three-point implement control system with automatic compensation for changing draft loads with implements was invented by Irishman Harry Ferguson. He had partnered early with Englishman David Brown to build the Ferguson-Brown tractor. When the partnership didn't work out, Ferguson sold Henry Ford on the idea and they quickly struck a gentleman's agreement to build a new tractor incorporating the Ferguson hydraulics.

1939 Farmall F-20

When International Harvester introduced its Farmall in 1924, there was just the one model. The principles behind the Farmall proved so solid that IHC expanded the line, and by 1932, the original model was known as the Regular and was accompanied by a bevy of different versions for different sizes of farming operations. The F-20 was one of the best known due to its powerful 16/24 hp rating. Owner: Tom Hill of Piqua, Ohio. (Photograph by Ralph W. Sanders)

1940s: Pastoral scene
An Oliver 77 plies a field, planting corn on a sunny spring day as a herd of contented cows looks on. (Photograph by J. C. Allen & Son)

The first joint-venture 9N tractor rolled off the assembly line in June of 1939 and more than 10,000 tractors were sold that year. The "9" meant 1939 and "N" was the Ford designation for the tractor. To hold the price to around $600, parts from Ford car and truck assembly lines were used on the tractors. The tractor proved popular, but World War II material shortages and rationing meant low tractor inventories. The designation was changed from 9N to 2N (for 1942) to reflect simplified changes and to get around the War Production Board's price controls.

Following the war, Henry Ford Sr. was forced out and his grandson took over the company controls. Faced with nosebleed-sized losses, the decision was made in 1946 to disband the tractor partnership with

Harry Ferguson. The younger Ford soon figured out Ferguson was the only one making any money in the deal. Ford had built tractors at a fixed price for Ferguson, who then sold tractors and equipment to farmers through his Ferguson dealers, one of which was located in Pontiac, Michigan. As a young kid, I remember sitting with Dad in the Ferguson tractor dealership—actually the garage behind the dealer's house in downtown Pontiac.

The Ford goal was to build a completely new tractor to go head-on with whatever tractors Ferguson could piece together. By 1948, Ford offered a line of implements under the Dearborn Motors Company name. I remember seeing farm magazine ads for Dearborn Motors farm machinery. Since the city of

1952 Farmall Super C

Style came to farm tractors in 1938 as Deere hired noted industrial designer Henry Dreyfuss to give a facelift to its straightforward working machines. Not to be outdone, International Harvester brought on Raymond Loewy to streamline its Farmalls. The curvaceous Farmall A was one result; it evolved into the Super C by 1952 and was an ideal machine for truck gardeners and smaller farms. (Photograph by Keith Baum)

Dearborn was the home of Ford Motor Company, it wasn't hard to figure out this tie-in with the new farm machinery arm of the Ford organization.

By then, Ferguson had developed the Ferguson TE-20 for Europe and soon followed with a plant in Detroit to build the TO-20 American version.

In late 1946, Harry Ferguson sued Ford for $251 million. Because Ford would no longer provide tractors, he felt he earned these dollars for loss of business and patent infringement.

Yet the real bone of contention was the hydraulically controlled three-point system, the only point on which Ferguson eventually won in court. This led to a court settlement of $9.25 million, much less than what Ford paid lawyers on the case.

Most importantly, Ford was required to come up with a new hydraulic system by 1953. This led to the decision to have Ford engineers design a better hydraulic system and to launch the new Jubilee tractor in 1953. Even as a teenager, I could tell that the tractor featured a pretty darned close copy of the Ferguson three-point hydraulic system. But it somehow withstood later court deliberations.

When we switched to baling hay in 1954, the Farmall Super H tractor was needed for PTO horsepower. Plus the PTO shaft of the Ford Jubilee tractor simply wasn't high enough off the ground to handle the baler's power needs.

With higher engine displacement and more power

than previous H model tractors, the Super H wasn't manufactured for long by International Harvester. It was introduced in 1952 and production was halted in 1954.

These H series tractors were advertised by International Harvester as a "two-plow tractor in any field." They were probably International's best-selling full-size tractor with more than 350,000 sold from 1939 to 1954.

The completely revised 1939 tractor design better served the changing needs of the American farmer. Features included increased horsepower, more reliability, and utility. New manufacturing materials provided longer life and many engine improvements were made.

The H tractor was a 1939 replacement for the much-loved International F-20 tractor. In 1940, you could buy a Model H tractor for $962 with rubber on all four wheels. This cost $172.50 more than tractors that came with four steel wheels— something many farmers had to settle for during the early 1940s when rubber was in short supply during World War II.

By 1954, the "letter line" was discontinued and replaced by the "hundred" series of bright red tractors. Yet there's much more to International's role in the tractor field at that time than just changing the way tractor models were named.

In hindsight, unfortunate business moves by International in the mid-1950s probably brought an end to the company's dominance of the U.S. tractor market. Branching out into construction equipment, home appliances, and other products meant the company was short of much needed investment and manufacturing funds. This soon led to the company falling behind the U.S. market in the one area which made the company great—production of those bright red tractors.

1947 Ford 2N

Henry Ford revolutionized farming not once but twice. The first was marked by the arrival of his Fordson tractor; the second came in 1939 with the debut of his 9N tractor. The 9N featured engineering principles such as Draft Control, the three-point hitch, and an implement system created by irascible Irishman Harry Ferguson but worked into production due to the acumen of Ford engineer Harold Brock. The 2N followed in 1942 as an economical wartime model. Owner: Titus Keller of Buffalo Springs, Pennsylvania. (Photograph by Keith Baum)

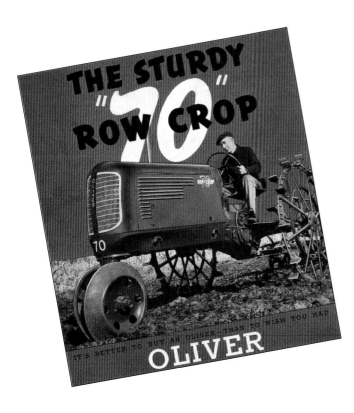

1930s Oliver 70 brochure

Above: *"It's better to buy an Oliver—than wish you had,"* *promised this brochure for Oliver's famous Model 70 Row Crop.* *Mounted on Oliver's Tip Toe Wheels, the 70 was one of the* *most stylish streamlined tractors in the 1930s.*

1938 Allis-Chalmers Model B

Right: *To do battle in the fields with International Harvester's* *Farmall F-12, Allis-Chalmers unleashed its small Model B in* *1938. Due to their one-plow scale and myriad uses, both trac-* *tors found a welcome niche among garden farmers and as a* *lightweight tractor for chores. And both tractors are still popular* *with collectors today. Owner: Dwight Hart of Jackson, Ten-* *nessee. (Photograph by Ralph W. Sanders)*

Chapter 4

The Golden Days of Harvest Time

"I loved threshing. It was like the Taj Mahal of farm work. It lasted long enough. It just lasted the right amount of time that you all had a lot of fun. It wasn't harder than any other kind of farm work. It was hot, sweaty, and dirty. It took a lot of chewing tobacco. I miss it."
—Samuel Stoltzfus, farmer from Lancaster County, Pennsylvania, 1999

Threshing days hold a special place in the heart of old-time farmers. It was a time of hard work that appeared as though it would never end. At the same time, it was a social event on the farm with few rivals, except Thanksgiving and Christmas. Threshing brought neighbor families together to share labor and a good meal—and, ultimately, to share the rewards of the farm life, as the cooperation on threshing day ensured that each and every family reaped the harvest.

Threshing was a chore that placed tractors on a pedestal as they powered the threshing machinery. The sound that the engines of the Johnny Poppers and Fords and Farmalls made in concert with the rattling percussion of the Case and Rumely and Woods Bros. threshers was a raucous symphony that symbolized another successful harvest.

1900s: Threshing days of yore
Main photo: *A threshing crew halts in its labors to pose for a prairie photographer's camera on the Canadian plains. (Glenbow Archives)*

1990s: Still going strong
Inset: *Two engineers operate a steam tractor at the Rough and Tumble Thresherman's Reunion in Lancaster County, Pennsylvania. (Photograph by Jerry Irwin)*

The Harvest

By Jerry L. Twedt

Jerry L. Twedt was born and bred on a farm in rural Roland, Iowa. In his remembrance of things past, *Growing Up in the 40s: Rural Reminiscence*, he writes in evocative and colorful prose of his childhood days down on the farm. His reminiscence resurrects the aura of a time when farmers had one foot firmly planted in ages-old traditional values while the other foot was poised to step into the atomic age. It was a time when family farms and family values seemed as permanent as a great red barn—a time that sometimes now seems sadly to be gone with the wind.

The world has moved from the Industrial Age to the dawn of the Computer Age, and much has changed in agriculture during the intervening years. Still, as Twedt writes, the golden days on the farm will forever be bred into a farm family's bones.

For eleven months of the year, it slept beneath the branches of a large, sprawling tree. It was quiet, and despite its monstrous size, ignored. Oh, small boys occasionally crawled up on it and pretended it was everything from an aircraft carrier to a spaceship, but, by and large, it was afforded no thought or consideration. During the winter, huge snow drifts surrounded it. And in the spring, its heavy steel wheels sank into the mud.

But in July, when the grain was heavy on thin yellow straws, a large tractor or a massive steam engine would awaken it from its slumber by pulling it from beneath the shade out into the brilliant Iowa sun. Chains and belts were taken from safe winter quarters and placed upon the conglomeration of drive pulleys and gears. Grease cups were filled and oil was generously squirted on any metal part that moved. Finally, the massive main drive belt, measuring over fifty feet in length and a foot in width, was unrolled and attached to the machine's drive wheel. After a twist was put into the belt, the other end was placed on the flywheel of the tractor or steam engine. The power source was then backed up until the belt was off the ground and taut. Slowly the flywheel began to rotate. With an almost painful groan, the giant machine's moving parts broke the bonds of nearly a year's neglect. Wheels turned. Shakers shook. Gears ground. Faster and faster the flywheel turned, until the monster was in full cry, its jagged metal teeth lashing out to lacerate the imaginary grain. It was threshing time.

For the next month, all attention was focused on the threshing machine as it prowled the countryside, devouring bundles of grain into its bowels. This prairie dinosaur frightened the horses, petrified small children, worried wives and mothers, and fascinated young boys, and, like the dinosaur, is now extinct.

Threshing was the final act of a three-act production. The first act was sowing the grain, which in our case was oats. Very little wheat was grown in Central Iowa.

. . . Once the cutting and shocking were done, the threshing machine was pulled from its winter quar-

1933: Helping hand
A Wisconsin youth cranks over the engine on his family's Case tractor in the days before starter motors became common accessories. (Photograph by J. C. Allen & Son)

ters, and the final act of the harvest began. A threshing run (why it was called a "run" is a question I cannot answer) usually consisted of between ten and fifteen farms. According to my father, a rule of thumb was to have ten men hauling bundles, two manning the oats wagon, and one managing the machine. If the run were too small, the operation was inefficient due to the lack of manpower. But, if the run were too large, weeks could go by before a farmer's grain was safely in the bin.

Generally, each farmer owned a share of the threshing machine; however, one man was selected to operate it. He was the only man on the run who did not have to furnish either a hay rack or an oats wagon. He was also the acknowledged leader and arbiter of disputes. To small boys, being in charge of the threshing machine was one of the life's ultimate achievements, and rare was the farm boy who did not picture himself at some future date in this lofty position.

On our run, Uncle Leonard was the man. My most vivid mental picture of Leonard is one of him standing on top of the threshing machine, much like a captain on the bridge of a ship. His felt hat, which he wore winter or summer, is cocked so that it almost touches his left ear; his knees are flexed to absorb some of the machine's vibrations; in one hand is a long-stem oil can and in the other a roll of belt paste; and on his face is an intense expression of concentration as he looks and listens for the first sign of trouble. To me, he personifies the threshing boss.

A threshing machine in operation was an impressive sight. Most were roughly twenty feet long, six feet wide, twelve feet high, and made of thin sheet metal. Some of the older models were smaller and had wooden sides. On the front of the machine was a hinged feeder, onto which the bundles were unloaded. In this feeder, measuring about six feet long and a yard wide, was a conveyer system composed of wooden cross pieces attached to two flat link chains. Projecting from the cross pieces were nail-like points of steel, which assisted in keeping the bundles moving into the machine. A board divided the feeder lengthwise, permitting unloading from either side.

As the bundles entered the machine, they were attacked by a row of cleaver-like blades. The bundles were torn apart, and the straw and oats fell into the heart of the machine, which consisted of series of shaking screens. Here the oats were detached from the straw

and channeled into the oats well. From the well, the grain was augured up to the top of the machine where it was funneled into the long cylindrical spout which augured it out into the wagon. The straw was dumped into a blower cave and then blown by a large exhaust fan out of the cave, through a long telescoping spout onto a pile or into a barn.

Next to the knives at the mouth of the machine, the blower cave was the most dangerous part of the

threshing machine. Naturally, this made it of special interest to small boys. Since the fan-shaped hatch which opened into the cave had a latch on the outside, it made a great dungeon when the machine was not in use. Lying in the semi-darkness of the blower cave (my feet braced against the small rim that divided the cave from the large fan) was eerie and a little frightening. I often thought of Pinocchio being swallowed by the whale.

1900s: Threshing crew

A threshing crew gathers before the steam engine that modernized their job on the Canadian prairies. The American-Abell steamer was built by the American-Abell Engine & Thresher Company of Toronto, Ontario. These steamers were later known by the moniker "Cock O' the North," a colorful nickname for the hard-laboring giants. (Glenbow Archives)

1910s: Threshing team

A threshing crew stands proudly beside its steam engine. (Minnesota Historical Society)

During the noon break, older boys used to love daring a younger boy to crawl into the blower cave. They called him "chicken," "scaredy cat," and "baby," until the boy agreed to do it. Then the conversation went something like this:

"You . . . you won't lock the door?"

"Nahhh, we wouldn't do that."

"You're sure?"

"Sure we're sure! We wouldn't think of locking it, would we fellows?"

"No!"

"Well . . . OK, but just for a little bit."

Once the boy had slid into the cave, the hatch was slammed shut. Immediately, the boy began to yell. The older boys laughed and started yelling things like, "It's threshing time!" or "Start the tractor up, Joe!" Hearing this, the boy panicked and began to cry and pound on the hatch. If the older boys were extra mean, they might even push the starter button the tractor. After a proper amount of pleading, the boy was let out and admonished, under fear of death, not to tell any adult. But, he usually talked, and the affair earned the older

boys some time stacking straw or threats from their fathers to "kick their hind ends up between their shoulder blades!"

The job everyone hated on a threshing run was stacking straw. To do the job properly, there was no way of avoiding the chaff and the stinging pieces of straw from the spout. As in shocking, it was necessary to wear a long sleeve shirt outside of the pants. It was also a good idea to keep the collar button fastened, the collar turned up, and wear goggles. No matter what precautions a man took, there was no way to keep from getting filthy dirty.

The worst part of stacking straw, however, was not the dust and chaff; it was the lack of moisture in the mouth and throat. After only minutes on the stack, your mouth felt like it was filled with cotton balls. It became almost impossible to swallow. Many methods of conserving the mouth's moisture were tried. The favorite means was chewing tobacco. My dad, when he was about seventeen, decided to see how the tobacco worked. He took a big chew in his mouth, climbed up onto the stack, and began to work. He chewed and he spat. He spat and he chewed. And, you know what? It worked. He did not have a dry mouth that entire afternoon. Of course, he did not stack any straw either. After ten minutes of chewing and spitting, he turned green and spent the rest of the day lying under the shade of a tree.

Until around 1940, the power source for the threshing machine was the steam engine. According to old timers, much of the romance went out of threshing with the demise of the steamer. I came along too late to have actually worked with one, but I remember, as a small boy, how awed I was by the pressure gauges, fire box, whistle, and the great, rear, steel wheels. Large tractors, usually an "M" Farmall, "A" John Deere, "Oliver," or "Minneapolis-Moline," took the place of the steamer. Although not as colorful, the tractor was more maneuverable, much more dependable, and given enough gasoline, would run all day with little attention. Some old farmers look back on the steamer with a good deal of nostalgia, but at the time of the changeover, there were few who mourned its passing.

No matter what the power source, or how big the threshing machine, neither was of much use until the grain was brought in from the field. For this we used the common, ordinary hayrack. As any modern farmer knows, the hayrack is no longer common or ordinary, but in the 1940's no farm was complete without one. For those not acquainted with hayracks, imagine a flatbed trailer about sixteen feet long and ten feet wide, with a floor of one by twelve's spread about an inch apart. Add to this three feet high frames on all four sides. The frames were constructed of one by sixes bolted to the vertical two by sixes, which in turn fit into slots attached to the bed of the rack. Think of a wooden fence like you see around horse farms built onto the bed. The four sides of the hayrack made up what farmers called "the basket." A ladder, three feet wide and nearly seven feet tall was added dead center in the front of the basket. The ladder made it possible to climb up onto the load when the farmer was finished. Many hayracks also had the back of the basket built up to a height of seven or eight feet. When fully loaded, this rather odd looking vehicle carried an amazing number of bundles.

Loading bundles was an exacting craft, bordering on an art form. Many an improperly loaded rack arrived at the threshing machine minus half of its original contents. To load bundles, you first filled the basket, then began stacking bundles, straw end out in rows along the two long sides of the rack. In effect, you were building two retaining walls of bundles. You erected one side, then the other, then tossed bundles into the middle. By following this procedure, and if properly executed, the top of the load would be about fifteen feet high. Since a solid load of bundles was generally the creation of one man working without the aid of

---

Grandpa and the Allis-Chalmers
By Mike Dolinski of Selkirk, Manitoba

Grandfather was really quite an old gentleman, a pretty hardened Swede from the coal mines. But he had arthritis quite bad, and to try and ease the pain, he used to soak his hands in hot wax. Because of this problem he sometimes had a lot of trouble operating machinery—especially getting his legs going if he'd been sitting for a while and gotten pretty stiff. My father one time put him on the tractor to do some cultivating. We had one of these small Allis-Chalmers tractors with the cultivator that was pulled behind. He got going out there that day, and he hadn't really left himself much room at the end to turn. He came to the corner where he was going to turn around, and he just wasn't ready for it and went straight into the bush. With that type of cultivator he had no way to back up, so there he sat in the bush.

My father, as his habit was with Grandpa, came driving out there at this particular moment to check to see how Grandpa was doing. And here was my Grandpa—he never wanted my dad to know that he'd made a mistake—with a little pocketknife, trying to cut away this tree so he could get himself out of this predicament he was in.

I remember he had the same sort of situation happen with the half-ton truck. He was going to come around this corner, and I don't know what happened—he got excited or something. But instead of hitting the brake, he got the gas pedal and drove us right into a big pile of rocks and made pretty good work of the oil pan on the truck.

1920s: "The Reapers"

Artist Ogden Pleissner's oil painting of two farmers reaping their grain evoked the feel of an autumn harvest day. (The Minne-apolis Institute of Arts)

anyone up on the load, a strong back, a certain feeling for proportion, and a good three-tine pitchfork were essential.

I officially joined the threshing run when I was twelve. My job was to drive the horses while my brother, Pete, loaded bundles. The team of horses was old and wise. I was neither. What I was, was excited! I wanted Jim and Lady to be the best team on the run. They had no such aim. Each had pulled countless loads of bundles and in no way shared my excitement. They responded to my commands at an exasperatingly slow gait. No matter how I yelled or threatened, they moved along at their chosen rate, showing complete contempt for my driving ability. When I complained to Dad, he laughed and said that neither one was capable of going faster than a slow trot. A few days later, I was to find out differently.

Pete and I were finishing a field on the Johnny Johnson farm. It was nearly dinner time, and we lacked only a few bundles of having a load. I was in my usual place, standing near the top of the ladder and leaning against the top board. There suddenly was the crunching sound of nails breaking free of wood, and before I knew what had happened, I found myself sprawled on the top of the wagon tongue between the two horses. To say Jim and Lady were frightened would rank among the great understatements of all time. In a moment, their fear transformed them from tired, spiritless draft horses into racing stock!

Down the field we went as fast as they could run. Although I was busy hanging on, I did notice that bundles were flying every which way. Poor Pete! He saw his carefully stacked load disintegrate before his eyes.

I had fallen squarely onto the wagon tongue and, although shaken up a little, was not hurt. As the horses ran, I wrapped my legs and one arm around the tongue and grabbed unto the back of Lady's harness with my free hand. I knew if I fell from the tongue, I would be stepped on by Jim and probably run over by the rack.

The danger of the situation was not my chief concern. In fact, things happened so quickly that I was not really frightened. But I was worried about losing the entire top half of the load. Being stepped on did not bother me. Being yelled at by Pete for losing his load, did! My first thought was to grab the reins. They were within reach, but snatching at them would have meant letting loose of either the tongue or the harness, and I was not about to do either. The only thing I could think of was to try and calm the horses by talking to them.

"Whoa, Jim . . . Whoa, Lady," I said in what I hoped was a reassuring voice. "Easy now . . . take it easy . . . whoa there."

Whether it was my voice or the simple fact that they had run farther in thirty seconds than they had in the previous fifteen years, the team slowed and came to a halt. I crawled out from behind the horses and looked at the load. It was a mess. The bundles, which had not fallen off, would have to be pulled off and restacked. I thought for sure I was in for a royal chewing out from Pete. About that time, Pete came running. But instead of being angry, he looked scared to death.

"Are you ok?" He panted.

"Yah, I think so."

"What happened?"

"I don't know. I was just standing on the ladder and then fell onto the tongue."

We both looked up at the ladder and saw that the top board was missing. It was only then that I realized what had happened.

"You're sure you're ok?" Pete asked again. "Do you think you can drive?"

"Sure, I'm ok." I said, more than a little surprised by Pete's mother hen anxiety. Pete and I had a very normal big brother, little brother relationship, with all of the fights, arguments, and tears that that relationship entails. But I also secretly believed he was the greatest big brother in the world. So, his obvious concern meant something special to me.

That evening when we arrived home, I told Dad about my fall and how fast Jim and Lady had run. He, like Pete, realized what might have happened. I was sent off to bed while he worked long into the night tearing apart the old ladder and replacing it with a new one on which the cross pieces were bolted to the uprights.

As a boy grew older, there was a natural progression from driver, to spike pitcher, to having a rack of his own. The intermediate step of spike pitcher was an apprenticeship in learning how to load bundles properly. The "spiker" would help a farmer load his rack, then, when finished, move on to another rack which was just beginning to load. Spiking was actually harder work than having one's own rack because there were

no rest periods while waiting to unload. The spiker also had a problem keeping up with the older man. Most spikers, were in their early teens, which made it very difficult to match the stamina and strength of the rack owner. Many men, myself included, live with back problems due to attempting to load too fast and pitch too high.

Before a young man was considered worthy of having his own rack, he first had to prove he was mature enough to unload into the threshing machine. There was no escaping the fact that this was dangerous work, and a threshing boss had to have faith that the boy was capable of pulling up to the machine and balancing on top of a load before he was allowed even close to the machine. My time came, quite by accident, when I was sixteen.

I was standing by our old Regular Farmall tractor, which had replaced Jim and Lady in pulling the rack, when the rack up at the machine finished unloading and pulled out. Dad's rack was up next, so I began looking around for him. He was nowhere in sight. The threshing boss (we had moved to a different farm and he was not my Uncle Leonard) motioned for me to pull up to the machine. It was a hot day and I had been sweating freely, but at that moment I really began to sweat.

The threshing boss motioned again. Still no sign of Dad. I knew I could not just stand there. All the other farmers waiting in line were looking at me. They realized it was my time for testing. I took as much time as possible cranking the Regular into life, hoping that Dad would arrive. He did not.

Guiding a big hayrack loaded with bundles to within a few inches of a threshing machine feeder was no easy task. Perhaps because of beginner's luck, I pulled the rack snugly up to the machine. This gave me a great shot of confidence because I had seen others hit the threshing machine or come in so far away, they had to pull out and make another pass. I crawled off the tractor and, once again, looked for Dad. He was not around.

My throat was dry, and my heart was pounding as I climbed the ladder. I had helped Dad unload before, but only after he had topped the load and there was little danger of falling. Standing by myself on top of a full load, fifteen feet high, was a whole different ball game! The hungry mouth of the threshing machine had never looked so menacing. I had heard stories of men falling into the feeder, but for the first time, saw

1915 Aultman Taylor 30/60

The Aultman & Taylor Machinery Company of Mansfield, Ohio, first offered its monstrous gas-fueled 30/60 in 1910, and it soon earned the undaunted respect of farmers everywhere for its reliability in powering threshing machines. The four-cylinder engine's bore and stroke measured an amazing 7.00x9.00 inches (175x225 mm), making each piston about the size of a coffee can. The massive machine remained the firm's flagship until the company was purchased in 1924 by Advance-Rumely; Rumely was in turn bought in 1930 by Allis-Chalmers. Owners: Mel and Lois Winter of Minneota, Minnesota. (Photograph by Ralph W. Sanders)

1900s: Thresher art

Stylish logo from the side of a threshing machine of the Robert Bell Engine & Thresher Company of Seaforth, Ontario. Along with its threshers, Bell imported into Canada several lines of tractors that were repainted and rebadged as Bell machines. These included the 12/24 from the Kinnard-Haines Company of Minneapolis, Minnesota, and the Imperial Super-Drive, which originated from the Illinois Tractor Company of Bloomington, Illinois. (Photograph by Andrew Morland)

1910s: Thresher art

Colorful logo from a threshing machine built by the J. I. Case Threshing Machine Company of Racine, Wisconsin. In a show of Wisconsin pride, Case's logo was highlighted by "Old Abe," the bald eagle mascot of a Wisconsin unit of the American Civil War. (Photograph by Andrew Morland)

1980s: Harvest time

A lone farmer aboard his Deere 4320 cuts corn on an autumn day. (Photograph by William H. Johnson)

how easily it could happen.

The threshing boss yelled at me, and I began to slowly and carefully pitch bundles into the feeder. There are few times in my life when I have concentrated as hard as I did then. Before long, however, the load was half gone, and Dad was climbing into the rack to help me finish. He did not say anything, but a broad grin on his face told me I had done well. A few days later, when we threshed at our farm, Dad took care of the oats wagon, and I was given my own rack.

With the exception of stacking straw, minding the oats wagon was the dirtiest job on the run. The oats spout on the threshing machine did not telescope. This meant a great deal of hand scooping was required to keep the oats from flowing out of the wagon. This was especially true when the wagon was nearly full. Many times my father yelled at me for letting the oats overflow. Add the heavy back work to the noise, the chaff, and the oats in your shoes, and it became obvious why

taking care of an oats wagon was less than loved.

But it was for this grain the farmers had worked since spring, so the oats were carefully scooped or elevated into bins where they were stored for feed. Few farmers in our area sold their crop outright. If the yield was good, it was a happy farmer, who, after the run had moved to the next job, could look at his large straw stack and bulging bins and know that his animals had feed and bedding for the long winter ahead.

Whenever old threshers get together, one topic is sure to be talked about with a great deal of eye rolling and lip smacking . . . the food! I am sure I have never eaten as much or as well as on a threshing run. It was like having Sunday dinner everyday of the week.

There was nothing fancy about the meals. But, hungry men who had been pitching bundles for five or six hours had no need and less desire for fancy food. A typical noon meal consisted of a menu such as this:

boiled or mashed potatoes; a vegetable or two, usually sweet potatoes, green beans, scalloped corn or creamed peas; some sort of salad, often home grown leaf lettuce with a sugar and vinegar dressing; meat, generally pot roast, pork chops, ham or chicken; homemade bread; and all topped off with freshly baked pie. What a feast! Supper was less extravagant. There was potato salad, cold cuts or meatballs, a salad, a vegetable, bread, and fruit for dessert. It was still a hearty meal, but nothing to match the dinner.

To prepare such sumptuous meals required a Herculean effort on the part of the farm wife. Even so, it was impossible to do it alone. When her turn came to feed the threshers, she would call in a half dozen of her relatives and neighbors to help prepare the food. In return, she would go to their farms to assist them. This was not only necessary, but also made the hard work more enjoyable.

On threshing morning, Mother was up and baking by four o'clock. By five-thirty, when Dad called me, that indescribable aroma of baking bread had infiltrated every room of the house. Mother stopped her baking long enough to get us breakfast, then she and my sister, Herma, started on the pies. Around eight, the other women arrived with extra place settings and serving bowls. After a little socializing, it was time to peel the potatoes, wash the lettuce, shell the peas, and do the hundred and one things necessary for a successful meal. By eleven o'clock, the women were running in three directions at once. Eleven-thirty found the kitchen in complete chaos! But, by twelve noon, the tables were set, the meat was done and everything was ready. What makes it all the more remarkable was that the meal was prepared on an old-fashioned cook range, with the temperature outside ninety degrees in the shade.

Promptly at noon, the threshing machine was turned off, and the men, with their stomachs growling in anticipation, trooped toward the house. Since no woman would allow fifteen to twenty filthy men to wash in her house, wash basins were set up beside a galvanized washtub of water in the back yard. The men also preferred washing outside because they could splash and slop around as much as they wanted. Never has cleaning up for a meal been so enjoyable.

I first removed my shirt, then lathered myself from the waist up. To rinse, I cupped my hands and splashed on water, taking a perverse delight in being as messy as possible. When I was finished, I dumped any remaining dirty water out and refilled the basin with more cool clean water. I put my face only a few inches from the basin and, again with cupped hands, drenched my face, neck, and shoulders. The cool water ran down my back and chest producing brief moments of sensual delight.

No farmhouse in our part of the state had enough table space to seat twenty men, so two shifts were necessary. Whether you ate first—which was by far preferable because while the second group ate, you could lie under a tree and rest—or second, depended largely on whether your rack was full or empty. A man with an empty rack was always in the first group to eat. This was so he could quickly return to the field for another load. What every bundle hauler strove for was to pull into the yard, see two or three loaded racks in front of him, and then have the threshing boss shut down the machine for dinner. Not only could he take as much time as he wanted to eat, he could have a good snooze afterwards! However, no matter when you ate, the food was guaranteed to be delicious.

A threshing table, if the run were going well and the weather was holding, was alive with boisterous, good spirits. There was much laughing and talking and teasing of the women, who were kept busy rushing from the dining room to the kitchen, filling empty bowls and platters. Often, to the delight of the boys and consternation of their fathers, the conversations were filled with stories of past runs. Even though somewhat embarrassing at times, the stories were good fun. They also provided the boys an opportunity to see their fathers as human beings, rather than just as parents.

Oddly enough, the dinner that stands out in my memory was not due to the food or the conversation, but to the drink. I had just turned sixteen that summer. I stood about six-foot-one and, perhaps, weighed one-hundred-forty pounds if I wore a heavy, winter coat. On that particular, hot, July day, we were threshing at the farm of an elderly couple. We had all been seated for dinner, and the woman of the house was pouring the liquid refreshment. The boys were all getting milk, and the men were asked if they wanted coffee or ice tea. I fully expected a glass of milk, but when she got to me, she asked, "Ice tea or coffee?" I am sure she thought I was retarded by the way my mouth dropped open. All I could think of was that she had asked me what I wanted. She thought of me as a man instead of a boy! The woman asked me again, and, since I couldn't stand coffee and had never tasted ice tea, I mumbled, "Ice tea." I looked at the amber liquid flowing into my glass and began to wonder what I had done. I reasoned, anything that looks that good must taste good, so I took a small sip. It was delicious! I then proceeded to drink three glasses, and would have had more had Dad not begun to give me funny looks. I walked out of that room ten feet tall!

Because of the great quantities of food consumed at a threshing dinner, it was necessary to rest for a few minutes following the meal. The men would lie down on the grass in the backyard or lean up against a shade tree and smoke. The boys, on the other hand, would roll around on the grass as if they were about to die of overeating. However, within a few minutes, one boy would steal another boy's hat, or a game of tag would be started, or someone would take a basin of water left over from washing up and dump it on an unsuspecting victim. No matter how it started, the boys always ended up running, shouting, laughing, and in a mass wrestling match. It was not unusual for a boy to be hungry again before the afternoon's work had begun.

By one o'clock, the men and boys were back at work. The women, after eating their dinner, were relaxing over a cup of coffee and praying that the threshing would be over by mid-afternoon. If that happened, they only had to prepare a lunch, rather than a warm meal. The lunch usually consisted of coffee, lemonade, and cookies or cake. One such lunch, in 1942, will always be remembered by my mother.

Some of the men had moved on to the next farm to start loading, but most were still at our place when the tractor was turned off and the threshing machine was prepared for the road. The men came up to the yard for lunch, leaving the horses untethered. No one gave this a second thought as the main object in life for most draft horses was to move as few muscles as possible.

My younger brother, Paul, was almost two years old, and my sister, Herma, and I had been assigned to watch him while Mother and the women served the men. As any child will tell you, watching a younger brother or sister is a dreadful bore. It wasn't long before Herma and I were playing, and Paul was nowhere to be seen. We didn't even miss him until one of the farmers pointed to the front gate and said, "Look at that!"

Everyone turned to see Dick and Dave, my dad's team of horses, plodding toward us. Behind, dressed only in a diaper and rubber pants, was brother, Paul. He held the reins in his hands and was running to keep up with the horses. As he reached the yard gate, he pulled on the right rein, and obediently the two horses, who each weighed well in excess of one thousand pounds, turned toward the fence.

"Whoa!" Paul shouted.

The horses stopped and Paul stood there grinning from ear to ear. Mother was standing on the front porch during all of this, a look of shocked horror on her face. While the men cheered and clapped for Paul, Mother darted off the porch. Never before or since have I seen her move so fast. She scooped Paul up in her arms and carried him into the house.

I would just as soon not say what happened to Herma and me after the threshers had gone.

The worst part of the threshing was doing the chores when we got home after a day's work. No matter how tired Dad and I were, we still had to slop the hogs, feed the chickens, pick the eggs, and milk the cows. Many a time, I put my head against the warm flank of a cow and dozed while my hands stripped her of her milk. Once finished, I took a sponge bath in the kitchen sink (we had no indoor plumbing) and fell into bed. No sleep-inducing pills were necessary after a full day on a threshing run.

In 1952, Dad and Uncle Les pooled their money and bought a combine. That was the end of threshing for me. At the time, there were a few small runs still struggling along, but by the mid-1950's, the threshing run had become a part of Americana.

For most farms, the day the combine arrived was considered a happy day. The farmer could harvest grain when he wished and did not have to wait his turn to thresh. The combine was far more efficient, requiring two or three days to do the work that formerly took two or three weeks. To the farm wife, it meant feeding two men rather than fifteen to twenty men. In short, it was a step forward . . . progress. But, progress always exacts a cost. Threshing forced people to be interdependent. The farmers and their wives had to work together, help each other, and share problems. There was no escaping the need for joint effort. What resulted was a sense of community . . . people who knew and cared for each other. It is sad that much of this sense of community has also become a part of American History.

1915 Russell 30/60

Above: *The towering 30/60 built by Russell & Company of Massillon, Ohio, was christened with the nickname "Giant" by the firm, an obvious allusion to the size of the machine but also speaking of its power and ability to run a thresher. Russell ceased operation in 1927, becoming one of the famed "orphan" makes. Owner: University of California–Davis. (Photograph by Ralph W. Sanders)*

1910s Case Thresher brochure

Right: *"Profit by Better Threshing" was the promise of this colorful brochure from the Canadian branch of the J. I. Case Threshing Machine Company.*

Rites of Passage

By Ben Logan

These days, novelist and filmmaker Ben Logan lives in New York City, but he remains rooted to the southwestern Wisconsin farm where he grew up.

Logan's memoir of his family's farm, *The Land Remembers: The Story of a Farm and Its People,* is a rare book. His writing is poetic and evocative of all that is good—and difficult—about life on the farm. Through his colorful anecdotes and well-crafted stories, he draws forth images that create an indelible sense of place—and a sense of belonging.

This excerpt from *The Land Remembers* recounts a special day when the young Ben Logan made the passage from childhood to become a member of the threshing crew.

 In a farm family without girls, each boy in turn helped in the house. Because I was the youngest, I worked with Mother longer than any of my brothers. There weren't any younger sons to take over and free me to work in the fields with Father.

At threshing time, until I was about twelve, my work had to do with meals. Mother made her plans—getting ready for as many as twenty-five men—and I helped her put them into action. I carried extra water, brought in fresh vegetables from the garden, carried canned fruit up from the cellar, sliced loaf after loaf of the bread she had been up half the night to make. I peeled great pans of potatoes from the bin in the cellar, or dug new ones from the potato field. I got all the extra leaves from the dark closet at the foot of the stairs and soon the dining-room table stretched almost from wall to wall, lined with chairs from all over the house.

I set up buckets of water, washbowls, and great stacks of towels on the outdoor work stand, under the dinner bell. I made certain the stock tank was filled with water for the horses from the bundle wagons.

The roar of the threshing rig and the rattle of the wagons were constant reminders of men building up a hunger. Finally, the table was set, extra dishes stacked and ready for the men who couldn't fit at the first table. Pots bubbled on the wood range and good smells began to come from the steamy kitchen.

Then I began going back and forth between Father and Mother. The conversation would go like this, with a lot of running in between:

"Mother wants to know when you'll be ready?"

"When will she be ready?"

"She says the potatoes need forty-five minutes."

Father might call to the man on the last bundle wagon in line. "Hey, how many loads left out there?" He'd get his answer and turn back to me.

"We got this field about whipped. Then we have to move across the road. Ask her if we could eat early?"

"But she says the potatoes need forty-five minutes."

"Ask her about that."

"He says could they eat early?"

"Well. Maybe I can cut the potatoes up smaller. Tell him twenty minutes."

"She says twenty minutes. And she wants to know if they'll be eating here for supper."

"I don't know yet."

1930s: Rite of passage
Sporting their favorite beanies, two Indiana farm youths stand proudly at the wheel of their father's John Deere Model A tractor after learning how to plow with the Johnny Popper. (Photograph by J. C. Allen & Son)

"She said if you said that to ask you when you will know."

With the exact time set, Mother shifted her pots and pans, making sure everything came out even. And Father knew when to keep the empty wagons from going out for another load.

With the men beginning to look at their watches more often and measuring the height of the sun, the tractor would slow, the great belt slapping, and the hum of the threshing machine would slowly die.

In the strange warm quiet, after hours of steady sound, the men came to the yard, flapping chaff and dust from clothes and hats. They smelled of horses, grease, and grain dust, clothes stained with sweat and salt. Their straw hats made a pile on the grass. Once a puppy chewed some of them up while everyone was eating.

Four at a time, the men went to the washbowls, splashing and snorting like walruses, then rearing up, eyes full of soap, to feel for a towel. Every year, at least once, someone would hand a groping man a grease-filled rag brought in from the machines. The half-blind person would mop himself, not knowing anything was wrong until his face was black and a roar of laughter surrounded him.

Then to the house. Big, heavy bowls began to move around the table, forks spearing meat, potatoes, vegetables—sometimes a fork coming across from the other side of the table. One person was always the butt of all the jokes about eating too much.

"By God, George" (or "Tom," or "Spike," or "Dingy"), "we've been talking about you. What we decided is we ain't going to change work with you any more. Nothing personal, mind you. Just can't afford it, you eating ten times what the rest of us do."

"He could bring his own dinner."

"Hell, to do that he'd have to bring two wagons."

George would go on shoveling, talking through the food. "You're right. I do eat ten times as much as anybody else. No argument about that. Figure I got it coming, seeing as I work *twenty* times harder."

A hoot of laughter. The bowls made a second round. George speared a potato, popped the whole thing into his mouth and couldn't talk, eyes bulging as if he might explode. Still working on the potato he filled his plate with dessert, taking pie, cake, Jell-O, and cookies.

The chairs scraped back from the first table. The men went out to the yard, sprawling under the maple tree, to light pipes and hand-rolled cigarettes or take a chew from a plug of tobacco.

The second shift came in, heavy eaters sometimes taking a quick look into the kitchen to make sure there was plenty of food. I scurried from kitchen to dining room with more bowls of hot food, more bread, more coffee. I refilled the sugar bowl, put it down in front of a fat man, and waited while he put half the bowl over freshly sliced tomatoes and the other half into his coffee, running it over into the saucer. With the cup in one hand, he lifted the saucer and drank with a loud, vibrating slurp. Each time, someone at the table would rise to the occasion, frowning, looking under the table and saying, "Damnation, sure sounds like there's pigs and a slop trough in here somewhere."

The fat man grinned, handed me the empty sugar bowl, and went on eating. I kept circling the table, grabbing the bowls and platters as they emptied. I carried more cream and milk from the cellar, the pitchers steaming as they came up into the hot summer day.

Finally, with the food almost gone, the tractor started up, calling the men back to work. Mother and I sat down at the great long table, not talking, sobered by a mountain of dirty dishes waiting and another meal to be ready in five hours.

Father joined us sometimes for a consultation. Would the threshing be finished today? That might mean supper should be earlier than usual or later. Did we need anything from town?

When a job was going to be finished during the day, the women got nervous. Would the men eat at this job or move on to the next one, thresh an hour, and eat there? The women needed a definite answer. The men hedged. A tractor could break down, some wet bundles plug the machine, the last load slide off a wagon and have to be pitched back on.

In a situation like that, my liaison trips between Father and Mother seemed like every five minutes and the telephone rang with questions from a woman who might, or might not, have to feed twenty-five men two hours from now.

It wasn't talked about much, but there were farms where the men tried to avoid eating. They might quit a little early and decide everybody should go home to eat. They might decide to eat early at the present job.

I remember eating once at a house with no screens on the windows. The flies were a constant hum over

1929 Rock Island FA

Tractors bearing the name of the Rock Island Plow Company of Rock Island, Illinois, owe an allegiance to the small but well-respected Heider Manufacturing Company of Carroll, Iowa. Rock Island had signed on the dotted line to distribute Heider's machines. When sales soared, the small Iowa firm couldn't keep pace, so Rock Island purchased it. Rock Island continued to build tractors in the Heider mold until 1937, when the J. I. Case Company of Racine, Wisconsin, purchased the works. Owner: Dick Bockwoldt of Dixon, Iowa. (Photograph by Ralph W. Sanders)

Learning to Drive

By Bill Toews of Red River Valley, Manitoba

The first time I drove the tractor was in the spring operation. We were getting the land ready for seeding, and I was pulling a big disker. Of course this was a new tractor, one of the bigger tractors in the area at the time, so it had a special thrill for me.

I went home very excited and told my mother, who was horrified at the fact my father let me on the tractor at that age. But in fact my father had started one of my older brothers off on a tractor in a very horrifying way as well. When he was about ten years old, my father put my brother on an open-wheeled John Deere tractor with the hand clutch and told him to take the tractor into town. The thing he didn't do was tell him how to stop the machine.

So as he was going into town, my brother, who was a little absent-minded, suddenly realized that he had to figure out how to stop this thing in a hurry. And he found the hand clutch, but he couldn't pull it back because he was a little too light and a little too small. So he ended up bouncing off a couple of trucks and finally into a car before the tractor came to a halt.

the table. We ate with one hand and waved flies away with the other. Ben Twining had brought some repair parts for the tractor from Gays Mills. He made the mistake of staying for supper. When it came time for dessert, he reached out for a pie, saying, "I think I'll have some of that raisin pie."

A swarm of flies rose as his hand came near. "Oh," he said, "I guess that's custard pie."

One year I began the passage from boy to man. We were short of help because another threshing rig was over on Pleasant Ridge, where we usually exchanged help. Father said he needed me. Mother made plans for a neighbor girl to come and help.

"What will I do?" I asked Father.

"I was thinking about the straw pipe. Think you could handle that?"

"Sure." I had a dim impression of cranks and levers.

"It's not easy. You have to pay attention every minute. Couple years back I saw a boy knock a man off the strawstack being careless how he swung the pipe. You got to stick to it no matter how hot it gets, how much dust and chaff comes back at you."

"I can do it."

The rig came in the late afternoon, a big chugging Rumely Oil Pull tractor with a square stack and a little

1929 Cockshutt–Hart-Parr 18/28

Facing page, top: *Many Canadian agricultural firms established a tradition of importing American-made tractors that bore their own nameplates and paint schemes and re-christening them as "Canadian Specials." Faced with the high cost of developing and producing its own machines, the Cockshutt Farm Equipment Company of Brantford, Ontario, followed this scheme in selling tractors from the Hart-Parr Company of Charles City, Iowa. Through the decades, Cockshutt also similarly imported Allis-Chalmers and Oliver Hart-Parr machines before being purchased by Oliver in 1962. Owner: Richard C. Brown of Harriston, Ontario. (Photograph by Ralph W. Sanders)*

1937 Minneapolis-Moline ZTU

Facing page, bottom: *Minneapolis-Moline's vaunted Z Series of tractors made their debut in 1937. The Z was the premiere of the firm's Visionlined machines with new styling allowing the driver to better see over the hood. The Z was also the first Minne-Mo to feature the firm's famous Prairie Gold-and-red two-tone color scheme. Owner: Virden Smith of Findlay, Ohio. (Photograph by Ralph W. Sanders)*

box where black oil squirted mysteriously through glass tubes. It chugged through the barnyard to a field northeast of the barn, pulling the bright red threshing machine behind it.

The driver was my familiar big, greasy overalled man. He started getting ready for the next day, leveling up the threshing machine by digging holes for some of the wheels to drop into, then lining up the tractor and stretching the long belt from tractor pulley to threshing-machine pulley. Around the tractor were red milk cans filled with gasoline, unpainted milk cans full of water, and great boxes of tools and spare parts.

The long pipe that carried straw from the machine to the stack was cradled along the top of the thresher. I climbed up to the little platform where the straw-pipe operator was supposed to stand. There were three cranks and a rope. I didn't know which did what.

The big man swung the grain chute out and walked back along the top of the rig. "You going to run the pipe?"

I nodded.

"Ever do it before?"

I shook my head.

"You can do it. Let me show you. This crank here raises the pipe up and down. This crank swings her back and forth. This one makes her longer and shorter. And this rope—that opens up a little door at the end of the pipe. Pull that, the straw goes shooting straight out the pipe. Leave it closed, the straw goes down onto the stack. Got that straight?"

I nodded.

"All right. Let's try her. Raise the pipe off the rig a couple feet."

I turned the crank. The pipe lifted up.

"Fine. Now swing her around."

I turned another crank. The pipe began to swing in a great half circle, making a groaning noise.

"Hold it." He picked up his oil can and gave the collar of the pipe a big squirt of oil.

"Try her again."

The pipe turned more easily and I swung it until it stuck straight out from the end of the thresher.

"Now get the feel of cranking her longer and shorter."

I did that, chain links rattling along the top of the pipe.

"You'll do fine." He winked at me. "Now then, put her back on top the rig the way she was. You can crank her around in the morning. Folks'll think you been doing it all your life."

In my mind I cranked that pipe half the night.

First thing next morning, when the dew was off, we went out into the fields to tip the oat shocks over, butts toward the morning sun so the dampness from the ground would dry out. As I worked, I remembered the first time I had ever done that. It had been early in the morning, the sun still low and red. In an hour or so I had to go back to the house and help Mother. I started tipping the shocks, the butts directly at the sun. Lyle was with me. He watched for a few minutes, then came over, shaking his head. "Nope. Not right at the sun. Tip them where the sun's going to be a couple hours from now."

I looked at the sun. I looked to the right along the horizon where I knew the sun was going. But how far to the right?

"Like the face of a clock," Lyle said. He pulled out the inch-thick old watch that bulged from the top pocket of his high-bibbed overalls. The hands stood at seven o'clock. He turned the face so the little hand pointed to the sun. He pointed his finger from the center of the watch to the number nine.

"That's where the sun'll be in a couple hours."

I went back to tipping the shocks, looking at the sun each time, aiming the butts at that certain angle to the right. I'd never before had such a feel of the sun's absolute route across our days.

That had been three years before. I turned the shocks casually now, automatically aiming them ahead of the sun.

The wagons, with their wide hayracks, began to arrive. I helped throw bundles—from shocks that had been tipped the day before—onto the first wagon and rode in on the high swaying load.

The tractor was already running. The wagon pulled in close to the feeder apron. I slid off and ran to the pipe—raised it, cranked it around in a half circle, then extended it. I gave the rope a couple of pulls, opening the little door and letting it clang shut. Everything went without a hitch.

I looked down and found Father watching me. There was surprise on his face. He looked at me a moment, then at the thresherman, then back at me. I nodded.

Father smiled his approval and I grew about two inches up there on that high platform.

Another wagon pulled in along the other side of the machine. The thresherman pulled the drive lever on the tractor. The threshing machine came alive under me, vibrating, rocking back and forth a little, the chaff dancing on the metal top. Slowly it all built to a steady humming that was half sound, half feel.

The men on the wagons began feeding oats to the machine, their pitchforks swinging in an easy alternating rhythm. A steady line of bundles was carried by the moving apron into the hidden workings of the great machine. The tractor engine roared louder. New sounds began as bundles were ripped apart and oat heads shook loose from the stems. Straw rattled under me and went shooting out the pipe. The oat grains sifted through screens and fanners and poured into the measuring bucket on top of the machine. The bucket filled to a half-bushel weight and dumped automatically, registering on the counting dial. Then the oats poured down the grain pipe in a rich stream to the waiting sack.

As always, Father was there to meet those first oats. He reached into the sack and brought out a handful, still warm from the fields, bright gold in the early sun. He blew into his hand, checking for chaff and weed seeds. Satisfied, he nodded to the thresherman.

Father went next to the beginning pile of straw. He held his hat out in front of the pipe, then checked in it to see if any grain was blowing through. Again he nodded his satisfaction to the thresherman.

Father returned to the grain pipe and carefully lifted a full bag up and down. This was how he confirmed what his walks through the fields had told him earlier. Everyone watched his face. As he swung the first bag into the waiting grain wagon, we knew without a word ever passing that it was a good crop.

The bundle wagons came and went. The grain wagon raced off to the granary to unload and return. Straw spread out on the ground in a long pile as I swung the pipe back and forth. Father and a neighbor moved into the straw, which was next winter's bedding for the barns. With their pitchforks they began to form the rectangular outlines of the stack, motioning to me when they wanted the pipe moved.

Once, straw stopped coming out of the pipe. The machine groaned and thumped. Someone yelled. I looked around. The thresherman was running toward me. He made a pulling motion. I grabbed the rope that opened the door at the end of the pipe, and a wad of damp straw went shooting out beyond the stack. The machine smoothed. After that, the sound warned me when to pull the rope.

The sun moved across the sky. The dust and chaff settled around me. Once, when the bundle wagons got behind, I had a minute to climb down to earth and get a drink of water from the ten-gallon milk can, like the other men.

Finally, it was time for dinner. The machine whined to a stop, my little platform strangely motionless after hours of vibration. Father slid down from the strawstack and gave me a nod and a smile. There was a burst of laughter from the grain wagon. Lyle lifted a baby rabbit out of one of the bags. "Look at that," he said to the thresherman. "Can't understand how your rig can get the oats clean if a rabbit can go straight through."

The thresherman grinned. "You're lucky. Few days ago a skunk came through."

Lyle put the rabbit down and it hopped away across the field. He told me later that somebody had found it under a shock and brought it in.

I beat the chaff and dust off my clothes and washed up with the other men. For the first time in my life, I sat down at the first table. Mother put a steaming platter of food in front of me.

When the chairs scraped back, I went out into the yard with the others. There, under the shade of the big maple tree, I listened to the talk.

"Call this grain?" a hired man was saying. "Hell, you should see it out on the Great Plains. They got wheat fields that stretch from hell to breakfast. I've seen twenty horses hitched onto one combine. A man starts cutting and by God he's got to take a bed with him cause he'll only be halfway around a field by nightfall."

There was laughter. "You sure you're not stretching things a little?"

"Hell no. If anything, I'm holding back 'cause I didn't figure anybody would believe the truth. Fact is, those fields are so big, and it takes so long to get the seed in, that different parts of the field don't even get ripe at the same time."

Old Abe was there. He was listening and nodding. "My grandfather was out there once. He came West from Ohio back in the eighteen-forties. Tried to grub out a farm down in Haney Valley. Somebody came by and told him he was crazy. Said there was land out on the Great Plains level as a table, not a tree in sight. Well, sir, he went out there and just about went crazy before he turned around and came back here."

"What went wrong?"

Abe took a chew of tobacco and got it going. "Why, he said a man used to hill country could lose his soul out there. Said that country swallowed you up without even a belch. Said there was no surprises. Country shows itself to you all at once. No privacy either. A neighbor living twenty miles away can look out in the morning, see if you're up and got a fire going yet."

Abe raised his head. A long stream of tobacco juice went sizzling into the brown grass. "So he came back here, my grandfather did. Said hill country had a feel of home about it, didn't keep leading a man off toward a horizon that was never there."

From that year on I was part of the threshing crew. When the rig went to the next job, leaving our farm quiet again and sleeping in the hot summer sun, I went with it to run the strawpipe at each farm along the ridge.

1990s: "Autumn Flush"

The arrival of combines, which combined power and harvester into one machine, put an end to threshing days on the farm. Iowa artist Charles Freitag captured the aura of an autumn harvest day in his painting of a team of farmers bringing in the corn crop with their Farmall 450 tractor and corn harvester. A Farmall M does its duty pulling grain wagons to the corn barn. (Apple Creek Publishing)

Charles Freitag

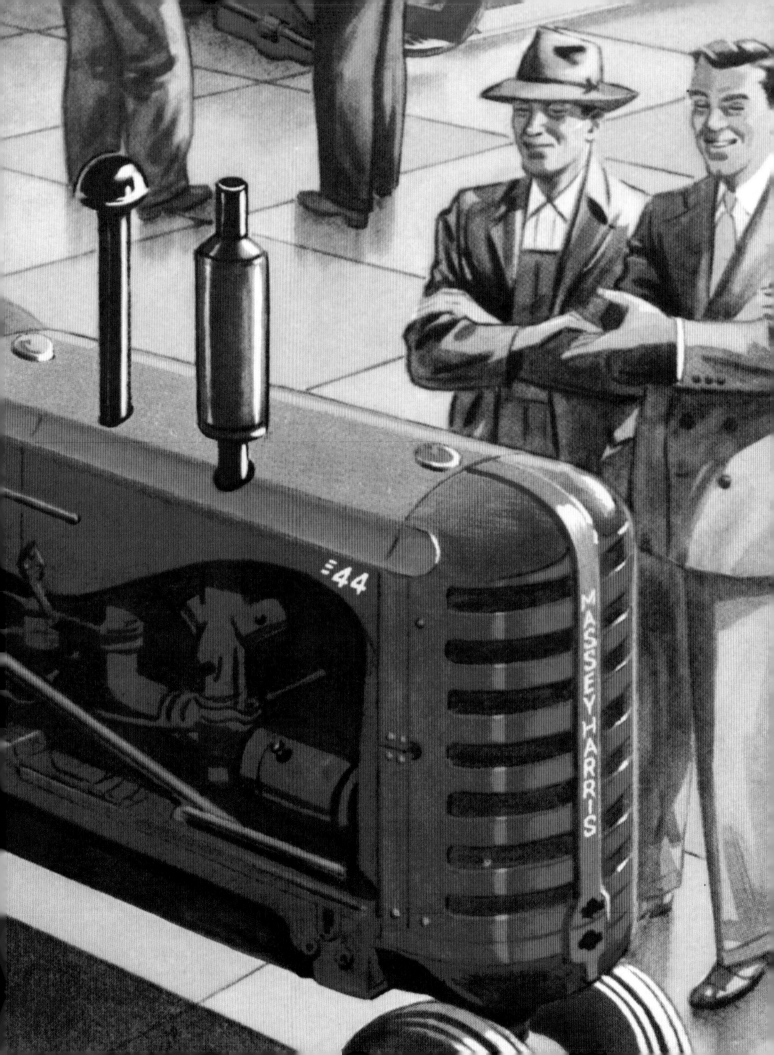

Chapter 5

Sold on Tractors

"The origin of the word 'tractor' was originally credited to the Hart-Parr Co., in 1906 to replace the longer expression 'gasoline traction engine,' which W.H. Williams, the company's sales manager, who wrote the advertisements, considered too cumbersome. The word actually was coined previously and was used in 1890 in patent 425,000, issued on a tractor invented by George H. Edwards, of Chicago."
—U.S. Department of Agriculture, *Power to Produce*, 1960

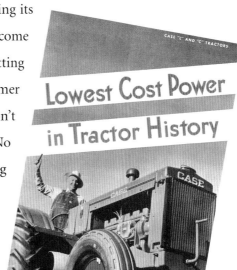

In 1923, International Harvester was field testing its radical new all-crop tractor that would soon become world famous under the name Farmall. After getting his turn behind the steering wheel, one Texas farmer proclaimed, "It's homely as the devil, but if you don't want to buy one you'd better stay off the seat." No one since has so succinctly summed up the feeling of being sold on tractors.

To some farmers, tractors were a necessary evil. To others, they were things of beauty. Whether the tractor endeared itself to them or not, everyone respected the work the tractor was capable of doing.

1950s: Sold on tractors
Main photo: *With World War II now history, the future looked bright in the 1950s. New tractors in brilliant new colors flooded the market and tractor sales soared, as depicted in this image from a* Massey-Harris Buyer's Guide. *Soon almost every farm in North America boasted one of the iron horses.*

1930s: Happy farmer
Inset: *This joyous farmer happily pilots his Case Model C on the cover of a 1930s Case brochure.*

304

ALEXANDER BOTTS
Earthworm Tractors

WILLIAM HAZLETT UPSON

Earthworm

BILL GILLIES

I'm a Natural Born Salesman

By William Hazlett Upson

The saga of tractor salesman extraordinaire Alexander Botts was created by writer William Hazlett Upson, who knew firsthand of what he wrote. Botts sprung from Upson's own experience working in the Holt Caterpillar Service Department from 1919 to 1924. "I spent a lot of time traveling around the country shooting trouble, repairing tractors, and instructing the operators," Upson wrote. "My main job was to follow up the salesmen and try to make the tractors do what the salesmen had said they would. In this way I came to know more about salesmen than they know about themselves."

Upson was born in New Jersey in the shadow of New York City, but he soon decided that instead of following in his father's footsteps as a lawyer, he would become a farmer. "Life as a farmer, I told myself, would be quiet, languid, and blissfully happy," Upson wrote. He enrolled in Cornell University to study agriculture, then bought a farm. After three years, he gave up farming, as it required so much work that he shuddered to think about it ever again.

Based on his time at Holt Caterpillar, Upson's stories about Botts and the fictitious Earthworm crawlers became so popular that he eventually penned 112 Botts tales between 1927 and 1975.

Here is the premier installment of Botts's adventures, which appeared in the *Saturday Evening Post* on April 16, 1927.

STONEWALL JACKSON HOTEL
MEMPHIS, TENNESSEE
March 15, 1920.

The Farmers' Friend Tractor Company,
Earthworm City, Ill.

GENTLEMEN: I have decided you are the best tractor company in the country, and consequently I am giving you first chance to hire me as your salesman to sell tractors in this region.

I'm a natural born salesman, have a very quick mind, am twenty-eight years old, am honest and reliable, and can give references if required. I have already had considerable experience as a machinery salesman, and I became familiar with your Earthworm tractors as a member of the motorized field artillery in France. I can demonstrate tractors as well as sell them.

When do I start work?
Very truly yours,
ALEXANDER BOTTS.

1920s: Earthworm tractors for sale
This was the first collection of Alexander Botts and Earthworm Tractors stories published in book form by William Hazlett Upson.

FARMERS' FRIEND TRACTOR COMPANY
MAKERS OF EARTHWORM TRACTORS
EARTHWORM CITY, ILLINOIS

March 17, 1920.

Mr. Alexander Botts,
Stonewall Jackson Hotel,
Memphis, Tenn.

DEAR MR. BOTTS: Your letter is received. We have no opening for a salesman at present, but we are badly in need of a service mechanic. As you say you are familiar with our tractors, we will try you out on this job, at $100 per month plus traveling expenses.

You will report at once to our Mr. George Healy, salesman for Tennessee and Mississippi, who is now at the Dartmouth Hotel, Memphis. You will go with him to Cyprus City, Mississippi, to demonstrate a ten ton Earthworm tractor for Mr. Jackson, a lumber operator of that place. Mr. Healy will tell you just what you are to do.

We enclose check for $100 advance expense money.

Very truly,

GILBERT HENDERSON,
Sales Manager.

STONEWALL JACKSON HOTEL
MEMPHIS, TENNESSEE

March 19, 1920.

The Farmers' Friend Tractor Company,
Earthworm City, Ill.

GENTLEMEN: As soon as your letter came, I went around to see Mr. Healy, and it is lucky for you that you hired me, because Mr. Healy has just been taken sick with appendicitis. They were getting ready to take him to the hospital, and he was pretty weak, but he managed to tell me that the tractor for the demonstration had already arrived at the freight station in Cyprus City.

He also explained that this Mr. Jackson down there owns about a million feet of Cyprus timber which he want to get out and sell right away before the present high price of lumber goes down. It seems the ground is so swampy and soft from the winter rains that with his present equipment of mules and wagons he won't be able to move any of his timber until summer.

But Mr. Healy was down there a couple of weeks ago, and he arranged to put on a demonstration to show Mr. Jackson that an Earthworm tractor can go into those swamps and drag out the timber right away. Mr. Jackson said he would buy the tractor if it did the work, and Mr. Healy was feeling very low because he was sick and couldn't go down to hold the demonstration.

"You can rest easy, Mr. Healy," I said. "When you look at me you're gazing on a natural born salesman. I will go down there and do your work as well as mine. I will put on a swell demonstration, and then I will sell the goods."

As Mr. Healy did not seem to know just what to say to this, I gathered up all his order blanks, selling literature, price lists, etc., and also the bill of lading and the check to pay the freight on the tractor. Then I wished him good luck, and left.

From this you can see that I am quick to grasp an opportunity, and that you made no mistake in hiring me. I am leaving for Cyprus City tonight.

Cordially yours,

ALEXANDER BOTTS.

FARMERS' FRIEND TRACTOR COMPANY
SALESMAN'S DAILY REPORT

Date: March 20, 1920.
Written from: Delta Hotel, Cyprus City, Miss.
Written by: Alexander Botts, Service Mechanic and Pinch Hitter Salesman.

I found this pad of salesman's report blanks among the stuff I got from Mr. Healy. I see by the instructions on the cover that each salesman is supposed to send in a full and complete report of everything he does, so I will give you all particulars of a very busy day.

I arrived at 7:51 this morning at Cyprus City— which turns out to be pretty much of a hick town in what they call the Yazoo Delta. The whole country here is nothing but a swamp, and the main street of the town ends in a high bank that they call a levee, on the other side of which is the Mississippi River flowing along about twenty feet higher than the town.

After alighting from the train, and after noting that it was a cloudy day and looked like rain, I engaged a room at the Delta Hotel. I then hurried over to the freight station where I found the big ten ton Earthworm tractor on the unloading platform. They had

New SPEED FACTOR in Farming

Low Pressure Tires Promise Possibilities for Expediting Field Operations Without Increasing Expenditure of Power

1930s: "New Speed Factor in Farming"

When Allis-Chalmers first offered pneumatic rubber tires in the 1930s, a revolution in farming arrived—not to mention a revolution in comfort for farmers! Firestone Rubber Company worked with Allis in developing tires for agricultural use, and by the mid-1930s, "air tires" were replacing the old steel-cleated wheels on everyone's tractors, except for certain diehard old-timers. This cartoon poked fun at rubber tires and the promises of "faster farming" that accompanied them. Truth was almost stranger than this cartoon, however: To promote the new technology, a rubber-tired Allis Model U toured North American county and state fairs with famed race-car driver Barney Oldfield burning up the oval horse tracks at speeds of more than 60 mph (100 kph).

dragged it off the car with a block and tackle. And when I saw that beautiful machine standing there so big and powerful, with its fine wide tracks like an army tank, with its elegant new shiny paint, and with its stylish cab for the driver, I will admit that I felt a glow of pride to think that I was the salesman and service mechanic for such a splendid piece of machinery.

(NOTE: Of course, as I said in my letter, I am an old machinery salesman. But the largest thing I ever sold before was the Excelsior Peerless Self-adjusting Automatic Safety Razor Blade Sharpener. I did very well with this machine, but I could not take the pride in it that I feel I am going to have in this wonderful ten ton Earthworm tractor.)

After paying the freight, I hired several guys from the town garage to put gas and oil in the tractor, and then I started them bolting the little cleats onto the tracks. You see I am right up on my toes all the time. I think of everything. And I figured that if we were going through the mud we would need these cleats to prevent slipping. While they were being put on, I stepped over to the office of Mr. Johnson, the lumber man.

(NOTE: This bird's name is Johnson—not Jackson, as you and Mr. Healy told me. Also it strikes me that Mr. Healy may have been fairly sick even as long as two week ago when he was down here. In addition to getting the name wrong, he did very poor work in preparing this prospect. He did not seem to be in a buying mood at all.)

As soon as I had explained my errand to this Mr. Johnson—who is a very large, hard-boiled bozo—he gave me what you might call a horse laugh. "You are wasting your time," he said. "I told that fool salesman who was here before that tractors would be no good to me. All my timber is four miles away on the other side of the Great Gumbo Swamp, which means that it would have to be brought through mud that is deeper and stickier that anything you ever seen, young feller."

"You would like to get it out, wouldn't you?" I asked.

"I sure would," he said, "but it's impossible. You don't understand conditions down here. Right on the roads the mules and horses sink in up to their bellies; and when you get off the roads, even ducks and turtles can hardly navigate."

"The Earthworm tractor," I said, "has more power

1930s Minneapolis-Moline Model Z brochure

Above: *Minne-Mo heralded its new Model Z Series as "The Last Word in Modern Tractor Design" due to its "Visionlined" restyling of the hood. To sell tractors during the Great Depression, everyone from Deere to International Harvester was rushing to update the look of their machines with a styling facelift. (Minnesota Historical Society)*

1990s: "Old Time Service"

Left: *Those were the days.... Once upon a time, the tractor dealer or repair person drove out to your farm with his handy box of tools and fixed your machine while you rested your bones in the shade. Iowa artist Charles Freitag's oil painting remembers such a day. (Apple Creek Publishing)*

than any duck or turtle. And if you'll come out with me, I'll show you that I can pull your logs through that swamp."

"I can't afford to waste my time with such crazy ideas," he said. "I've tried motor equipment. I have a motor truck now that is stuck three feet deep right on the main road at the edge of town."

"All right," I said, always quick to grasp an opportunity, "how about coming along with me while I pull out your truck?"

"Well," said Mr. Johnson, "I can spare about an hour this morning. If you'll go right now, I'll go with you—although I doubt if you can even pull out the truck. And even if you do, I won't buy your tractor."

"How about going this afternoon?" I asked.

"I'll be busy this afternoon. It's now or never."

"Come on!" I said.

We went over to the freight platform, and as the cleats were now all bolted on we both climbed into the cab.

(NOTE: I will explain that I was sorry that Mr. Johnson had been unable to wait until afternoon, as I had intended to use the morning in practicing up on driving the machine. It is true, as I said in my letter, that I became familiar with Earthworm tractors when I was a member of a motorized artillery outfit in France, but as my job in the artillery was that of cook, and as I had never before sat in the seat of one of these tractors, I was not as familiar with the details of driving as I might have wished. However, I was pleased to see that the tractor seemed to have a clutch and gear shift like the automobiles I have often driven, and a pair of handle bars for steering very much like those of a tricycle I had operated in my early boyhood.)

I sat down on the driver's seat with reasonable confidence; Mr. Johnson sat down beside me; and one of the garage men cranked up the motor. It started at once, and when I heard the splendid roar of the powerful exhaust, and saw that thirty or forty of the inhabitants, both white and otherwise, were standing around with wondering and admiring faces, I can tell you I felt proud of myself. I put the gear in low, opened the throttle, and let in the clutch.

(NOTE: I would suggest that you tell your chief engineer, or whoever it is that designs your tractors, that he ought to put in a standard gear shift. You can understand that it is very annoying—after you have pulled the gear shift lever to the left and then back—

to find that instead of being in low you are really in reverse.)

As I said, I opened the throttle, let in the clutch, and started forward. But I found that when I started forward, I was really—on account of the funny gear shift—moving backwards. And instead of going down the gentle slope of the ramp in front, the whole works backed off the rear edge of the platform, dropping at least four feet into a pile of crates with such a sickening crash that I thought the machine was wrecked and both of us killed.

But it soon appeared that, although we were both very much shaken up, we were still alive—especially Mr. Johnson, who began talking so loud and vigorously that I saw I need have no worry about his health. After I had got Mr. Johnson quieted down a bit, I inspected the machine and found that it was not hurt at all. As I am always alert to seize an opportunity, I told Mr. Johnson that I had run off the platform on purpose to show him how strongly built the tractor was. Then, after I had promised I would not make any more of these jumps, he consented to remain in the tractor, and we started off again.

(NOTE: Kindly tell your chief engineer that Alexander Botts congratulates him on producing a

1938 Graham-Bradley 501.103

Facing page, top: *The six-cylinder Graham-Bradley 20/30 tractor built by Graham-Paige Motors Corporation of Detroit, Michigan, was available by mail order to rural customers down on the farm. Introduced in 1938, it was offered through Sears Roebuck & Company of Chicago, Illinois, and was sold at Sears' retail stores or via its huge mail-order catalog. Graham-Paige was famous for its luxury automobiles, and the firm's beautiful tractor boasted streamlining that belied its heritage. This 501.103 row-crop tricycle model was available alongside the 501.104 wide-front that debuted in 1939. Both ended production in 1941. Owner: Vern Anderson of Lincoln, Nebraska. (Photograph by Ralph W. Sanders)*

1948 Co-op E3

Facing page, bottom: *In a rare twist of importing Canadian tractors to sell in the United States, the National Farm Machinery Cooperative of Bellevue, Ohio, marketed its Co-op Model E3 to American farmers. The Co-op machine was actually a Cockshutt Model 30 disguised by a new paint scheme and decals. To add to the confusion, the tractor was also sold by the American Gambles Stores chain as the Farmcrest. Cockshutt had factories in Brantford, Ontario, and Bellevue, Ohio, to supply its American neighbors. Owner: Midland Co-op of Stilesville, Indiana. (Photograph by Ralph W. Sanders)*

practically unbreakable tractor. But tell him that I wish he would design some thicker and softer seat cushions. If the base of the chief engineer's spine was as sore as mine still is, he would realize that there are times when good thick seat cushions are highly desirable.)

As we drove up the main street of Cyprus City, with a large crowd of admiring natives following after, I seemed to smell something burning. At once I stopped, opened up the hood, and discovered that the paint on the cylinders was crackling and smoking like bacon in a frying pan.

"Perhaps," suggested Mr. Johnson, "there is no water in the radiator."

I promptly inspected the radiator, and, sure enough, that was the trouble.

(Note: I would suggest that if your chief engineer would design an air-cooled motor for the tractor, such incidents as the above would be avoided.)

I borrowed a pail from a store, and filled the radiator. Apparently, owing to my alertness in this emergency, no damage had been done.

When we started up again, we had not gone more than a few yards before I felt the tractor give a little lurch. After we had got a little farther along I looked back, and right at the side of the street I saw one of the biggest fountains I have ever seen in all my life. A solid column of water about eight inches thick was spouting high in the air, spreading out at the top like a mushroom, and raining down all around like Niagara Falls.

I heard somebody yell something about a fire plug; and, as I have a quick mind, I saw right away what had happened. The hood of the tractor is so big that it had prevented me from seeing a fire plug right in front of me. I had unfortunately run right into it, and as it was of very cheap, inferior construction, it had broken right off.

For a while there was great excitement, with people running here and there, hollering and yelling. The sheriff came up and took my name, as he seemed to think I was to blame—in spite of the fact that the fire plug was in such an exposed position. I was a bit worried at the way the water was accumulating in the street, and consequently I was much relieved when they finally got hold of the water works authorities and got the water turned off. You see the fire mains here are connected to the Mississippi River, and if they had not turned the water off the whole river would have flowed into the business district of Cyprus City.

(Note: I would suggest that your chief engineer design these tractor hoods a little lower so as to avoid such accidents in the future.)

After the water had been turned off, we got under way again, clanking along the main street in high gear, and then driving out of town to the eastward over one of the muddiest roads I ever saw. The tractor, on account of its wide tracks, stayed right up on top of the mud, and rolled along as easy and smooth as a Pullman car. Behind us a large crowd of local sightseers floundered along as best they could—some of them wading through the mud and slop, and others riding in buggies pulled by horses or mules.

Mr. Johnson acted as if he was pretty sore—and I did not blame him. Although the various mishaps and accidents we had been through were unavoidable and not my fault at all, I could understand that they might have been very annoying to my passenger. Perhaps that is one reason I am such a good salesman; I can always get the other fellow's point of view. I livened up the journey a bit by telling Mr. Johnson a number of Irish jokes, but I did not seem to get any laughs—possibly because the motor made so much noise Mr. Johnson couldn't hear me.

By this time I had got the hang of driving the machine very well, and I was going along like a veteran. When we reached Mr. Johnson's truck—which was deep in the mud at the side of the road about a half mile from town—I swung around and backed up in front of it in great style.

The road, as I have said, was soft and muddy enough but off to the right was a low, flat stretch of swamp land that looked much muddier, and a whole lot softer. There were patches of standing water here and there, and most of it was covered with canebrake— which is a growth of tall canes that look like bamboo fishing poles.

Mr. Johnson pointed out over this mass of canebrake and mud. "That is an arm of the Great Gumbo Swamp," he yelled very loud so I could hear him above the noise of the motor. "Your machine may be able to navigate these roads, but it would never pull a load

1950s: Toy tractors at work
Selling real tractors sometimes also meant selling toy tractors to the kids. While Pa heads off to the fields to harvest the crops, the children practice farming on a smaller scale. (Minnesota Historical Society)

through a slough like that."

I rather doubted it myself, but I didn't admit it. "First of all," I said, "we'll pull out this truck."

We both got out of the tractor, and right away we sank up to our knees in the soft sticky mud. The truck was a big one, loaded with lumber, and it was mired down so deep that the wheels were practically out of sight, and the body seemed to be resting on the ground. Mr. Johnson didn't think the tractor could budge it, but I told him to get into the driver's seat of the truck so he could steer it when it got going.

By this time a gentle rain had started up, and Mr. Johnson told me to hurry up as the truck had no cab and he was getting wet. I grabbed a big chain out of the truck tool box, and told Mr. Johnson to get out his watch. He did so.

"In just thirty seconds," I said, "things are going to start moving around here."

I then rapidly hooked one end of the chain to the back of the tractor, fastened the other end to the truck, sprang into the tractor seat, and started the splendid machine moving forward. As the tractor rolled steadily and powerfully down the road, I could hear the shouting of the crowd even above the noise of the motor. Looking around, however, I saw that something was wrong. The truck—or rather, the major portion of it—was still in the same place, and I was pulling only the radiator. As I had a quick mind, I saw at once what had happened. Quite naturally, I had slung the chain around the handiest thing on the front of the truck—which happened to be the radiator cap. And as the truck was of a cheap make, with the radiator not properly anchored, it had come off.

I stopped at once, and then I had to spend about ten minutes calming down Mr. Johnson by assuring him that the Farmers' Friend Tractor Company would pay for a new radiator. I backed up to the truck again, and Mr. Johnson took the chain himself, and by burrowing down in the mud managed to get it fastened around the front axle. Then he climbed back into the seat of the truck and scowled at me very disagreeably. By this time the rain was falling fairly briskly, and this may have had something to do with his ill humor.

When I started up again, everything went well. The motor roared, the cleats on the tracks dug into the mud and slowly and majestically the tractor moved down the road, dragging the heavy truck through the mud behind it.

At this point I stuck my head out of the tractor cab to acknowledge the cheers of the bystanders, and in so doing I unfortunately knocked off my hat, which was caught by the wind and blown some distance away. At once I jumped out and began chasing it through the mud. The crowd began to shout and yell, but I paid no attention to this noise until I had reached my hat and picked it up—which took me some time, as the hat had blown a good ways, and I could not make any speed through the mud. When at last I looked around, I saw that a very curious thing had happened.

In getting out of the tractor I had accidentally pulled on one of the handle bars enough to turn the tractor sidewise. And in my natural excitement—the hat having cost me $8.98 last week in Memphis—I had forgotten to pull out the clutch. So when I looked up, I saw that the tractor with Mr. Johnson and his truck in tow, was headed right out into the Great Gumbo Swamp. It had already got a good start, and it was going strong. As Mr. Johnson seemed to be waving and yelling for help, I ran after him. But as soon as I got off the road the mud was so deep and soft that I could make no headway at all. Several of the bystanders also attempted to follow, but had to give it up as a bad job. There was nothing to do but let poor Mr. Johnson go dragging off through the swamp.

And, although I was really sorry to see it, Mr. Johnson going off all by himself this way, with no protection from the pouring rain, I could not help feeling a thrill of pride when I saw how the great ten ton Earthworm tractor was eating up that terrible soft mud. The wide tracks kept it from sinking in more than a few inches; the cleats gave it good traction; and the motor was so powerful that it pulled that big truck like it was a mere matchbox—and this in spite of the fact that the truck sank in so deep that it plowed a regular ditch as it went along.

As I am a natural born salesman, and quick to grasp every opportunity, I yelled a little sales talk after Mr. Johnson. "It's all right," I hollered; "I'm doing this on purpose to show you that the Earthworm can go through any swamp you got." But I doubt if he heard me; the roar of the tractor motor was too loud. And a moment later the tractor, the truck, and Mr. Johnson had disappeared in the canebrake.

While I was considering what to do next, a nice looking man in a corduroy suit came over to me from one of the groups of bystanders. "This is only an arm of the Great Gumbo Swamp," he said. "If that tractor doesn't mire down, and if it goes straight, it will come

1960s: One of the family

Above: *For many farmers, the tractor was almost part of the family. Farmers relied on their tractors to make a living, and the working relationship they developed was one of fondness and respect for a good machine. Here, a farm family pays homage to their Ford. (Minnesota Historical Society)*

1940s: State fair time

Left: *State and county fairs were prime time for tractor dealers to show off their wares as farm folk came to town in a sprightly mood. This poster announcing the Minnesota State Fair was even crowned by an image of a farmer on his brand new crawler—no doubt purchased on Machinery Hill. (Minnesota Historical Society)*

1950s: Tractor square dance

Both photos: *The Farmall Fast-Hitch Square Dance Kids toured North America performing their mechanized versions of the tried-and-true hoe-down at state and county fairs everywhere. Moving at a snaillike 3 to 5 mph (4.8–8 kph), the quartet of Farmall 200 tractors "danced" their repertoire of twenty basic square dance "steps." If this didn't sell you on the fleet-footedness and tight turning circle of the Farmall, nothing would. This really did happen. (Minnesota State Fair)*

out on the levee on the other side about a mile from here."

"An Earthworm tractor never mires down," I said. "And as long as there is nobody there to pull on the handlebars, it can't help going straight."

"All right," said the man, "if you want to hop in my buggy, I'll drive you back to town and out the levee so we can meet it when it gets there."

"Fine!" I said. "Let's go." I have always been noted for my quick decisions, being similar to Napoleon in this particular. I at once climbed in the buggy with the man in the corduroy suit, and he drove the horse as fast as possible into town and then out the levee, with all the sightseers plowing along behind—both on foot and in buggies.

When we reached the place where the tractor ought to come out, we stopped and listened. Far out in the swamp we could hear the roar of the tractor motor. It got gradually louder and louder. We waited. It was still raining hard. Suddenly there was a shout from the crowd. The tractor came nosing out of the canebrake, and a moment later it had reached the bottom of the levee, with the big truck and Mr. Johnson dragging along behind. As the tractor was in low gear, I had no trouble in jumping aboard and stopping it—and it is just as well I was there to do this. If I had not stopped it, it would have shot right on over the levee and into the Mississippi River, probably drowning poor Mr. Johnson.

As it was, Mr. Johnson was as wet as a sponge, on account of the heavy rain, and because he had been too cheap to get himself a truck with a cab on it. But he was a long way from being drowned. In fact, he seemed very lively; and as I got down from the tractor he jumped out of the truck and came running at me, waving his arms around, and shouting and yelling, and with a very dirty look on his face. What he had to say to me would fill a small book; in fact, he said so much that I'm afraid I will have to put off telling you about it until my report tomorrow.

It is now midnight and I am very tired, so I will merely enclose my expense account for the day and wish you a pleasant good night. Kindly send check to cover expenses as soon as possible. As you will see, my $100 advance is already gone, and I have had to pay money out of my own pocket.

Cordially yours,

ALEXANDER BOTTS.

EXPENSE ACCOUNT

Railroad fare (Memphis to Cyprus City)	$6.10
Pullman ticket	3.20
Gas and oil for tractor	8.50
Labor (putting on cleats, etc.)	9.00
36 doz. eggs at 50 cents per doz	18.00

(NOTE: It seems the crates we landed on when we dropped off the freight platform were full of eggs.)

1 plate glass window	80.00

(NOTE: I forgot to say in my report that in the confusion following the breaking of the fire plug I accidentally side-swiped a drug store with the tractor.)

Radiator for truck, and labor to install	46.75
Cleaning hat and pressing trousers	3.50
TOTAL	$175.05

(NOTE: I will list the hotel bill, the bill for the fire plug, and other expenses when I pay them.)

FARMERS' FRIEND TRACTOR COMPANY
SALESMAN'S DAILY REPORT
Date: March 21, 1920.
Written from: Delta Hotel, Cyprus City, Miss.
Written by: Alexander Botts.

I will take up the report of my activities at the point where I stopped yesterday when Mr. Johnson had just gotten out of the truck and was coming in my direction. As I stated, he had a great deal to say. Instead of being grateful to me for having given him such a splendid demonstration of the ability of the Earthworm tractor to go through a swamp, and instead of thanking me for saving his life by stopping him just as he was about to shoot over the levee into the Mississippi River, he began using very abusive language which I will not repeat except to say that he told me he would not buy my tractor, and that he never wanted to see me or my damn machinery again. He also said he was going to slam me down in the mud and jump on my face, and it took six of the bystanders to hold him and prevent him from doing this. And although there were six of them, they had a lot of trouble holding him, owing to the fact that he was so wet and slippery from the rain.

As I am a natural born salesman, I saw right away that this was not an auspicious time to give Mr. Johnson any sales talk about tractors. I decided to wait until later, and I walked back to the tractor in a dignified manner, looking back over my shoulder, however, to make sure Mr. Johnson was not getting away from the guys that were holding him.

After they had led Mr. Johnson back to town, I made up my mind to be a good sport, and I hauled his truck into town and left it at the garage to be repaired. The rest of the day I spent settling up various expense items—which appeared on my yesterday's expense account—and in writing up my report. When I finally went to bed at midnight, it was with a glow of pride that I thought of the splendid work I had done on the first day of my employment with the great Farmers' Friend Tractor Company, Makers of Earthworm Tractors. Although I had not as yet made any sales, I could congratulate myself on having put on the best tractor demonstration ever seen in Cyprus City, Mississippi.

This morning, after breakfast, I had a visit from the nice-looking man in the corduroy suit who gave me the buggy ride yesterday.

"I am a lumber operator," he said, "and I have a lot of cyprus back in the swamps that I have been wanting to get out. I haven't been able to move it because the ground has been so soft. However, since I saw your tractor drag that big heavy truck through the swamp yesterday, I know that it is just what I want. I understand the price is $6000, and if you will let me have the machine right away I will take you over to the bank and give you a certified check for that amount."

"Well," I said, "I was supposed to sell this machine to Mr. Johnson, but as he has had a chance at it and hasn't taken it, I suppose I might as well let you have it."

"I don't see why you gave him first chance," said the man in the corduroy suit. "When your other salesman, Mr. Healy, was down here, I gave him more encouragement than anybody else he talked to. And

1950s: Trying a tractor on for size
A farm youth assesses the ergonomics of the latest and greatest Minneapolis-Moline GB Diesel at the Minnesota State Fair's Machinery Hill. (Minnesota State Fair)

he said he would ship a tractor down here and put on a demonstration for me."

"By the way," I said, "what is your name?"

"William Jackson," he said.

As I have a quick mind, I saw at once what had happened. This was the guy I had been supposed to give the demonstration for in the first place, but I had very naturally confused his name with that of Mr. Johnson. There ought to be a law against two men with such similar names being in the same kind of business in the same town.

However, it had come out all right. And, as I am a natural born salesman, I decided that the thing to do was to take Mr. Jackson over to the bank right away—which I did. And now the tractor is his.

I enclose the certified check. And I have decided to remain in town several days more on the chance of selling some more machines.

Cordially yours,

ALEXANDER BOTTS.

———

TELEGRAM
EARTHWORM CITY ILLS 1015A MAR 22 1920

ALEXANDER BOTTS
DELTA HOTEL
CYPRUS CITY MISS
YOUR FIRST REPORT AND EXPENSE ACCOUNT RECEIVED STOP YOU ARE FIRED STOP WILL DISCUSS THAT EXPENSE ACCOUNT BY LETTER STOP IF YOU SO MUCH AS TOUCH THAT TRACTOR AGAIN WE WILL PROSECUTE YOU TO THE FULLEST EXTENT OF THE LAW
  FARMERS FRIEND TRACTOR COMPAXY
  GILBERT HENDERSON SALES MANAGER

———

NIGHT LETTER
CYPRUS CITY MISS 510P MAR 22 1920

FARMERS FRIEND TRACTOR CO
EARTHWORM CITY ILLS
YOUR TELEGRAM HERE STOP WAIT TILL YOU GET MY SECOND REPORT STOP AND THAT IS NOT ALL STOP THE WHOLE TOWN IS TALKING ABOUT MY WONDERFUL TRACTOR DEMONSTRATION STOP JOHNSON HAS COME AROUND AND ORDERED TWO TRACTORS STOP THE LEVEE CONSTRUCTION COMPANY OF THIS PLACE HAS ORDERED ONE STOP NEXT WEEK IS

Ignominous Arrival

By Palmer Fossum of Northfield, Minnesota

My first Ford tractor (guess I've had more than 250 of them by now) was a 1940 9N Ford-Ferguson. Actually, it was my Dad's as I was still pretty young. The pretty little gray Ford-Ferguson was delivered on a cold November day by the dealer, who brought it out on a flatbed truck. The dealer had assumed we had a loading platform, or at least a roadside bank to facilitate unloading the tractor. We had neither. Delivery of the new tractor seemed about to be completely frustrated when Dad spotted a frozen manure pile. The truck was quickly backed up to the heap and the Ford-Ferguson made a humble entry into our lives by driving right down the frozen muck.

TO BE QUOTE USE MORE TRACTORS WEEK UNQUOTE IN CYPRUS CITY STOP MASS MEETING MONDAY TO DECIDE HOW MANY EARTHWORMS THE CITY WILL BUY FOR GRADING ROADS STOP LUMBERMENS MASS MEETING TUESDAY AT WHICH I WILL URGE THEM TO BUY TRACTORS AND JACKSON AND JOHNSON WILL BACK ME UP STOP WEDNESDAY THURSDAY FRIDAY AND SATURDAY RESERVED FOR WRITING UP ORDERS FROM LUMBERMEN CONTRACTORS AND OTHERS STOP TELL YOUR CHIEF ENGINEER TO GET READY TO INCREASE PRODUCTION STOP YOU BETTER RECONSIDER YOUR WIRE OF THIS MORNING
  ALEXANDER BOTTS

———

TELEGRAM
EARTHWORM CITY ILLS 945A MAR 23 1920

ALEXANDER BOTTS
DELTA HOTEL
CYPRUS CITY MISS
OUR WIRE OF YESTERDAY STANDS STOP YOUR JOB AS SERVICE MECHANIC WITH THIS COMPANY IS GONE FOREVER STOP WE ARE PUTTING YOU ON PAY ROLL AS SALESMAN STOP TWO HUNDRED PER WEEK PLUS EXPENSES PLUS FIVE PER CENT COMMISSION ON ALL SALES
  FARMERS FRIEND TRACTOR COMPANY
  GILBERT HENDERSON SALES MANAGER

Another Dream Fulfilled

By Patricia Penton Leimbach

Patricia Penton Leimbach is farming's Erma Bombeck. Like Bombeck, she is a sage philosopher on the trials and tribulations of everyday life. She writes with a sharp pen about the joys and troubles, the hard work and humor, the meaning and value of rural living.

Leimbach was raised on a fruit farm near Lorain, Ohio. Alongside her husband Paul, a fourth-generation farmer, she has run End O' Way farm in Vermilion, Ohio, for more than four decades.

It is through her writing that Leimbach has become one of the best known farm women in North America. For many years, she authored the weekly "Country Wife" column in the Elyria, Ohio, *Chronicle Telegram* newspaper. She also has three books to her credit, *A Thread of Blue Denim*, *All My Meadows*, and *Harvest of Bittersweet*, all of which are filled with wit and wisdom culled from her firsthand knowledge of everything from raising puppies to driving truck.

In this essay, she celebrates the arrival of yet another tractor.

"Here comes your new tractor," said Paul, looking up from lunch and down the road in response to the dogs' barking.

"If it's all the same to you, I'd just as soon have a Mercedes Benz," I said, looking out to where the International dealer was passing in a red blur.

The timing couldn't have been worse. I had come home late for lunch from running errands in town to find Paul cooking a couple of hot dogs (a sure sign of a farm wife's failure). As I heaved a halfbushel of canning tomatoes up onto the counter by the sink, he started carping at me about some grievances that had nothing to do with me.

"Honey, if you're angry with the guy, go tell him. Don't take it out on me!"

It evolved that the mailman had arrived just ahead of me and the implement dealer with a tardy check from the commission house. Some of the melon receipts as reflected in the check hadn't covered the cost of the boxes we packed the melons in. And now came this big new liability.

Whether I'm to hold title to "my tractor" or just pay for it had not as yet been determined, but my perambulations among farm people have taught me that a growing number of farm wives are working at outside jobs to keep the machinery from being repossessed. I pulled on my barn coat and went out to where the implement dealer had just unloaded the thing.

Shiny and red it was, and so clean! Hard to imagine this showroom model up to its axles in mud and manure. Not difficult, however, to imagine the pride of a farmer riding thereon. And a farmer's wife could

1940s: Another dream fulfilled
Pa's faith in farming was renewed in this International Harvester advertisement by his discovery of the new Farmall.

cut quite a figure up there too on that adjustable, padded seat—with arms, no less. Wow!

"Well," I said sarcastically, not quite ready to surrender to this folly, "it's the right color, no doubt about that. But it doesn't have my name painted on it anyplace. And does it go with all that stuff out there that it's supposed to pull?"

A new tractor is like a new suit. The shirt and the tie, the hat and the shoes have to match—likewise, the plow, the cultivator, the front end loader, the mower, and so on. Paul assured me that this tractor would fit well into our "machinery wardrobe."

The International dealer got on it then and demonstrated how the front end loader could be simply removed by slipping the cotter pins and pulling a couple of bolts.

"There's something you should appreciate," said Paul, making veiled reference to a skirmish I once had with a tree that was camouflaged in Virginia creeper. I bent the old bucket all to heck.

" . . . and see here, Pat, it's got a Bosch carburetor—just like a Mercedes-Benz," we finished in unison, laughing.

Someplace toward the end of her second or third decade as a farm wife, every woman must wake up one morning, look wistfully out toward the tractors in the machinery lot, and say to herself, "Is this all there is?"

Of course it isn't! There are new pickups, new plows, new planters, new disks; augers, manure spreaders, sprayers, chisel plows, wagons, and if you are very zealous and faithful, one golden summer day you'll get a shiny new combine!

And when Fred dies and leaves you a wealthy widow, all the eligible old duffers in the county will come around and size up your machinery lot. Just make sure it's all in your name.

1957 Porsche 122 Diesel

The Porsche name is famous today for its racy sports cars, but company founder Ferdinand Porsche first won renown for his work developing the Volkswagen. After creating the "people's car," Porsche crafted a volksschlepper, *or "people's tractor." A handful of Porsche's tractors were built from 1938 into the early years of World War II; production was then revived in 1945. From 1949 to 1957, Porsche tractors were built by the German Allgaier firm, which was later acquired by the Mannesmann group, which continued building the machines into the 1960s. Owner: Dan Magness of White Hall, Maryland. (Photograph by Ralph W. Sanders)*

1930s: Starting young

Above: *Many a farm youth oversaw a fleet of toy tractors that were cast in iron to be miniature replicas of the machines Dad drove. This painting by artist Arthur Carl Bade featured Junior operating his own dealership.*

1953 International Harvester Farmall Super H

Facing page, top: *Like father, like son: The love for a specific brand of tractor was often handed down through the generations like a family heirloom. If Grandpa swore by a Farmall, then Farmall it was—often for decades to come. It was rare that a farmstead switched "colors," much to the chagrin of tractor dealers who believed they had a better product to offer. Usually a change in makes came only after a calamity had occurred, such as the day when the old Fordson broke down in mid-furrow when it was needed most. That could have been the last straw, and the farmstead may have sworn a new oath to Massey-Harris. Owner: Kevin Haarklan of Dane, Wisconsin. (Photograph by Andy Kraushaar)*

1920s: Sold on tractors

Facing page, bottom: *Everyone down on the farm was sold on tractors and begged for their chance at the wheel. Here, two farm girls trade turns piloting the family's Samson Model M and operating the binder. (Photograph by J. C. Allen & Son)*

Chapter 6

The Glory and Misery of Driving Tractor

Tractor salesperson: "With this new tractor you can do twice as much work."
Farmer: "I do plenty of work now. What the heck do I want with a tractor that makes me do twice as much?"
—1930s tractor joke

The coming of the iron horse often did allow farmers do twice as much work—whether they wanted to or not.

Tractors also had other—perhaps more subtle—foibles that tractor salespeople failed to point out. Tractors did not produce free fertilizer in the form of manure as horse, mule, and oxen teams did. In addition, many tractors could operate without complaint from sunrise to sundown on a single tank of gas; farmers thus had to forego the feeding and watering periods that their teams needed—and that allowed the farmer to take a quick nap in the welcome shade of a tree. After a long day doing twice as much work as before, sitting on a cast-iron seat, and staring down seemingly endless rows, a certain tired glaze came over a farmer's face. Driving tractor was hard work.

1920s: Time out from plowing
Main photo: *Nothing builds a mighty thirst in a farmer like long hours in a tractor seat watching the plow to make certain the furrow is running straight and true. (Photograph by J. C. Allen & Son)*

1950s: Swinging times on the tractor
Inset: *"Join the Swing to Massey-Harris" shouted this Massey Buyer's Guide, hinting that farming with Canada's finest tractor would be as easy as playing on a child's swing.*

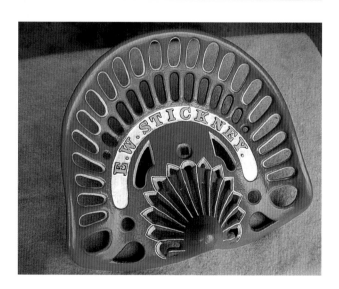

The Lowly Implement Seat: A Cinderella Story

By Orlan Skare

Orlan Skare was raised on a farm near Bagley, Minnesota, in the 1930s, earning his love for tractors and farm machinery firsthand. He went on to serve as a traveling salesman for International Harvester for six years. He then worked at Jostens before becoming a professor of marketing and sales at the Willmar, Minnesota, technical college.

After he retired, Skare began putting down on paper recollections of his farming youth as a way to pass them on to his children and future generations. This story holds a certain poignancy in his memory.

My fascination with farm machinery began early. As little more than a barefoot toddler, I followed Dad's horse-drawn grain binder, walking in the bullwheel track where the sharp stubble had been pressed down. The binder was an engineering marvel. With speed reduction and acceleration gears, the ability to convert rotary motion to oscillation motion, and automatic twine tying knotters, it employed almost every mechanical principle known at the time.

If there was an area where farm machinery engineers might have been less adequate it was in the design of the seats used on all types of horse-drawn implements. The early seats were made of cast iron, often incorporating the maker's name. Later they were stamped from sheet metal, but both had the common trait of being mounted on a stiff metal shank, which did little to absorb the shocks when traveling over rocks

and hard ground.

Worse, the seats were usually painted a dark color like McCormick red or John Deere green, heat-absorbing color choices. While the seat might be downright cold at the start of morning's work, after sitting in direct sunlight during the noon lunch break, this same seat could become hot enough to fry eggs! Modesty resulting from my early Lutheran upbringing prevents me from proving my point, but I suspect that someone viewing my bare backside might still find faint traces of "McCormick" burned lightly in reverse print.

Overnight rain brought another problem. While holes in the seat were supposedly designed to let rainwater run through, there were always some depressions which held just enough cold rainwater to provide a shock, then an uncomfortable hour or two until the trousers dried.

A problem for which we can't really hold the engineers responsible was that of designing a seat to ac-

1900s: Artwork

"Lowly" implement seats as art. These cast-iron seats once graced tractors and implements from makers as diverse as the Norwegian Plow Company, Black Hawk, Saint Paul Plow Company, the Swedish Grönkvists Mekverkstad, E. W. Stickney, and the Peerless from C. Russell & Company. (Photographs by Mark Skare)

commodate a population of diverse derriere dimensions. A mechanically adjustable breadth appeared to be impractical, so it appears that size was simply anyone's guess at creating a one-size-fits-all seat. The result was some small ones for the petite posterior, some larger ones for more ample bottoms, and then many others falling in between.

But fate has a way of compensating for past shortcomings. Many of the old cast-iron seats were ornate in design and lettering, and have become highly sought-after collector's items. Most cast-iron seats are from makers that no longer exist and are highly prized—and highly priced. Some with fancy filigree represent the best in advertising art of the period. Many collectors today have made painting of these seats an Agrarian art form, while others prefer to simply clean them and leave them in their original condition.

1920s: Old-time comfort

Once upon a time, a farmer's own gluteus maximus was the only cushion on the old-fashioned cast-iron tractor seats. To cure the farmer's ills, a whole industry of entrepreneurs sprang up like spring wheat to offer miracle cures, including everything from air-filled pillows to the "E-Z Seat Spring." As this ad promised, "Save them from that tired worn-out feeling that follows riding all day on rough ground."

1930s: Long days on the tractor
The thrill of learning to drive tractor soon gave way to the realization that sitting behind the steering wheel on that cast-iron seat in the blazing sun was not all it seemed from the ground. (Minnesota Historical Society)

Man Things

By Lauran Paine Jr.

Lauran Paine Jr. grew up on a farm and has a special place in his heart for tractors. He is enamored with the noise, power, mechanical workings, and simply the overall *feel* of tractors.

Along with tool belts, pickup trucks, meatloaf sandwiches, and crowbars, Paine includes tractors in his book of essays entitled *Man Things . . . Equal Time for Men.* As he writes in the introduction, "This is a book about man things, the things men like, think, and do. If you read between the lines, it says a lot about why men act like men. I don't know where I first heard the term, but my wife uses it all the time. Whenever I am doing something that I think is a lot more fun than she does, she says, 'Must be a man thing.'"

There are of course women who share men's fascination with tractors, and Paine's essay in no way dismisses their enthusiasm. His musings are simply a gushing celebration of his love for the mechanical mule.

 Tractors are generally man things. They are awesome. They are so powerful, so purposeful. You just love to run them. You sit up high, cradled with a steering wheel . . . and levers and pedals and buttons and toggles and power. You can see far, see dirt and mud and things that you can do. And on a tractor you can do them: move stuff, scrape, plow, plant, cultivate, push, pull, dig, mow, haul, carry, furrow, harvest, or just drive around in a big field on a warm day and look at the livestock. Or you can sit on the ground resting your back on one of the big rear tires and eat your lunch and gaze out at all the plowing you did that morning.

Tractors come in all sorts of sizes and shapes and colors, from large to small, from green, blue, red, and orange, to rust. It really doesn't matter, as long as it's a tractor. An old tractor, with rust here and there, a seat with the paint worn off, that has been earning a living for thirty years, and is still earning a living, is about as perfect a thing as there is on this earth. It is old, but it runs oh so smooth and does what it does well. Man, it makes you feel good just being there and sharing life with it. This tractor is forever and when you are on it you are forever, too. And the huge new tractors that pull an eight-bottom plow . . . wow! You just a-sittin' up there, one with the land, helping it produce. You are doing something, really doing something. And you can see the result of your work. Just look behind you and see all that rich soil being turned over and layered anew for nature to spawn its miracles. You can smell the soil and the power of the diesel. And you can feel the steady, rhythmic vibrations of the soul of the machine, working, pulling, working, working, working. And you are there on the tractor. Oh, it's good; it's *soooo* good.

Take a Caterpillar type tractor, it is different but just as awesome. When you are on one of those you are where you want to be. You are really purposeful.

1930s: Man things
A farmer at one with his machine. (Library of Congress)

You can't go on the asphalt or concrete of civilization. You are one with where you are. They are not fast and it doesn't matter, because they are so darn strong. They can push and pull like no other and you are their master, all nestled in the seat with great levers to operate and the thing does what you tell it to do. And you sit there with those tracks on either side of you, going around and around, kicking up dirt and dust, just doing their thing. No whining. No excuses. Just purpose. Doing stuff that matters. Yeah, cat-tractors make you feel good.

Tractors are dirty and that is good. You drive one and you come home dirty, dirt and dust everywhere, caked into every crevice of your clothes. When you come home after a day of tractor driving, you don't just feel like you've done something, you *look* like you've done something. You are lookin' good, *real* good. And your ball cap with the tractor logo and sweat stains on it has dust all over it, too. You can knock the dust off your cap by slapping it on your knee, but that's it. You can wash the clothes, but not the tractor ball cap. Never. Because when you have a dirty tractor-logo ball cap on while you're down at the feed store, you are *somebody*.

Then there is hangin' around people who like old tractors. They *like* things. It is fun being around people who like things. When you are around people who like things, they are less likely to bitch about things. Tractor people like things.

In a perfect world every man would have some land and a tractor. There would be a pile of dirt at one end of the land. In the morning, the man would go out and use the tractor front loader and pick up the dirt one scoop at a time and move it to the other end of the property. The next day he would move it back. Or he could just plow. Plow one way one day and another way the next day. That would be livin'. That would be a man thing.

I've often said to my wife—she usually just smiles back at me and nods—that I'd like to start a business called "Plowers Anonymous." It would be on a big plot of ground and men would come and rent a tractor and plow, or scoop, or dig, stuff like that. Hey, if I built it, they would come! Promise. Women would be allowed but it would mostly be men that came. Playing in the dirt is mostly a man thing. We could even have meetings.

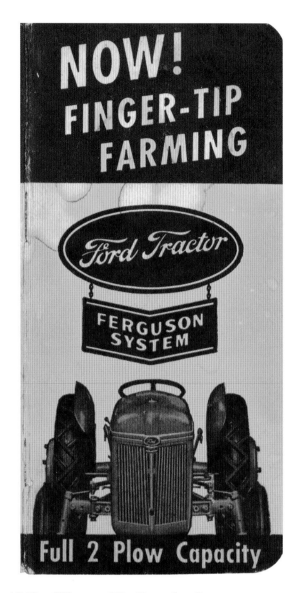

1940s: "Finger-Tip Farming"
Henry Ford and Harry Ferguson promised "finger-tip farming" with their Ford-Ferguson 9N and 2N tractors, as the cover of this little complimentary notebook stated. If it were only that simple!

Writing this has me all excited. If you buy enough of this book, I'm going to get another tractor. I think I'll drive it to work and the grocery store. Tractors are very acceptable, very in. They are not in *Vogue* or *Gentlemen's Quarterly*, but that's because it is understood they are cool. When you are on a tractor, you are not pretending to be anybody. You are just who you are and you are comfortable with that. Yeah, another tractor. A man can't have too many tractors.

1942 Massey-Harris 81

Above: *The pride of Canada, Massey-Harris's heritage stretches back to 1891. It was not until 1917 that the firm from Toronto, Ontario, first sold tractors, however, making it a relative late-comer to the power-farming field. The Model 81 made its debut in 1939 as a one-/two-plow machine and continued in production until 1948. The small workhorse won its share of fans over the years and formed the basis for a long lineage of smaller Massey machines. Owner: Ronald Hoffmeister of Altamont, Illinois. (Photograph by Ralph W. Sanders)*

1940s: Driving lessons

Left: *Pa gives Junior driving lessons before setting him loose on the family's International Harvester Farmall F-20. While Junior viewed it as a rite of passage and a newfound freedom, Pa was pleased to have added a new entry to Junior's list of chores. (Minnesota Historical Society)*

Charles Freitag

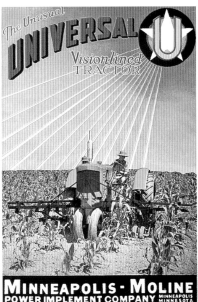

1930s: The glory of driving tractor

Above: *The rays of the sun appear to shine down like a halo upon this Minneapolis-Moline Model U working its way across an endless field on a blisteringly hot summer day. It was all only a trick of the graphic artist, however: "Visionlined" or not, a long day in the tractor seat was still a long day.*

1990s: "Oliver Twist"

Left: *A spectacular day aboard an Oliver 77 row-crop was the subject of Iowa artist Charles Freitag's oil painting ripe with all of the beauty of fall and vintage machinery. (Apple Creek Publishing)*

Chapter 7

The Allure
of Old Iron

"It's a strange thing, this Cult of Old Iron. I know better than to try to explain it to those who have not already been touched by it. Like any love, it's not a matter of logic, or research . . . not a process or a condition that can be explained. This passion is simply there—curious to the outsider, irresistible to the insider, mysterious to all."
—Roger Welsch, foreword to *This Old Tractor*

Vintage farm tractors seem to get better with age. It's certainly true that our memories of the old steel mules take on a golden patina with time. Nowadays, as collectors or enthusiasts or simply dreamers, we forget about the hot days in the field when the Oliver broke down just when we needed its help the most.

The allure of old iron continues to grow. Tractor buffs look back to the machines of their youth with sentimental longing, search out the rusty skeleton of an ancient Allis that was forsaken in a windbreak, or watch restored Farmalls rumble by during a show or parade and almost feel the need to salute. Long may these vintage machines live!

1954 Allis-Chalmers WD45
Main photo: *This Allis WD45 glistens with its fresh restoration and new coat of paint, a testament to the passion old iron can inspire. Owner: Little Britain Ag Supply of Little Britain, Pennsylvania. (Photograph by Keith Baum)*

1930s Minneapolis-Moline UDLX brochure
Inset: *"Hats Off to a Greater Modern Tractor by the Modern Tractor Pioneers" cheered this Minne-Mo brochure for its own UDLX. The self-praise took an ironic turn for the Comfortractor, however, as the tractor proved* too *modern for its age.*

The Virgin on the Farmall—The Venus in the Chevy

By Bill Holm

Bill Holm lives in the small Minnesota prairie town of Minneota, where he was born in 1943. Along with teaching at Southwest State University in Marshall, Minnesota, he has taught American literature at the University of Iceland in Revkjavik and at Xi'an Jiaotong University in central China. He is the author of several books of poems, including *The Dead Get By With Everything* and *Boxelder Bug Variations*, as well as a number of books of essays and prose, such as *The Heart Can Be Filled Anywhere on Earth: Minneota, Minnesota.*

This elegy to tractors and other machines on the farm comes from Holm's book of essays, *Landscape of Ghosts*, published by Voyageur Press. As he says half in jest in the book's introduction, it is a volume "full of pictures of stuff nobody wants to look at and of essays on subjects no one wants to read about." To too many folk, a rusted tractor is just that. To others, a tractor means much more.

 The measuring of an age in centuries and decades has become a kind of bad mental habit, a filing system gone berserk. We cut and trim history and reality to fit our generalizations so as to make neat sequences and invent catchy tags. The "twenties," the "roaring, dirty, thirties," the "wartime forties," the "sleepy fifties," the "revolutionary sixties"—or worse yet, the Age of Reason, the eighteenth century, as if in 1799, the central committee met to formally give up faith in reason and decide (as a committee might put it) to go into machines in a really big way. The metric or decimal division of history is frequently as graceless and inane as metric weights and measures. Imagine the metric version of these familiar phrases:

31.103 grams of prevention are worth .373 kilograms of cure; I love you 35.238 liters and 8.809 liters (a bushel and a peck); walk 1.609 kilometers in your neighbor's shoes before you judge him; .473 liters of beer, if you please, kind bartender.

A foot is not only a unit of measurement; it is attached to your body. A yard is not only three feet; it is where we all go to lie at last. History, too, goes awry when it loses its connection to our own bodies and to daily experience. One of the obligations of having been born with a brain and eyes is to make our own historical demarcations, our own tags, and then to put

1941 International Harvester Farmall Model B
Farmalls inspired faith in many farmers. The quality of restoration work on this Model B was a testament to the respect its owner had for the small steel workhorse. (Photograph by Andrew Morland)

them modestly before our neighbors in order to see if our experience touches theirs in enough ways to be worth thinking about.

To that end, as the twentieth century, or the second millennium, starts putting on its overshoes for the long trip into the night, I propose that we call this: The Age of Failed Machines, or The Age of Iron Litter. Drive down any farm road in Minnesota or anywhere in the Midwest, or for that matter, anywhere in America. Where trees grow at all, there's a small grove around the farmstead, sometimes only a few stray boxelders and cottonwoods, sometimes something more grand and orderly, usually the gift of the Department of Agriculture. The denser the grove, the harder you will have to look at sixty miles an hour, but trust me, reader, you will find it. In that grove, or behind the weathered corncrib or next to a rock pile, or in brazen places unashamedly visible in the front yard, sits the shrine of dead machines. There, in various conditions of rust, decay, and squalor lies a '49 Ford or a '53 Chevy, or an International truck, or a rotted manure spreader, or a hayrake with oxidized tines, or an F-20 iron tractor, or a drag, or a combine, or a plow. Sometimes there will be a little paint left so that you can tell a green John Deere from a red Farmall. Sometimes the car or pickup will be a wrecked heap, clearly towed to its final resting place. Sometimes it will have chugged in under the last power in its clotted cylinders, a favorite truck that finally gave up the ghost, took the last trip out back, and intends to go no further, at least in this world.

Machines and human beings have this in common: When age, broken parts, and advances in technology bring them to the end of their usefulness, you have to put them somewhere out of the way. They cease, to use eighties' language, to be viable; they can't work any more; it's too expensive to feed them or, even at a pittance a ton, to drag them down the road to the scrap-iron dealer. It costs more to move them those miles than to shove them into the grove and let them compost at their own pokey speed. For a while you might need a part or a bolt off their corpses, so you can visit them, crescent wrench in hand, and do a little recycling. But after a while even the bolt sizes change, and the rust is too thick. So in the lonely majesty of their graveyards, they wait for the second coming when old machinery shall be greased and oiled again in a glorified body.

How strange these metaphors of theology sound when used to describe old machines rusting in a grove. However ridiculous it seems at first, I ask you, dear reader, to think again, and to drive around the section or to the outskirts of town, and have a look. What you see back of the grove may be an American saint's relic, a shrine, a visible history of the rise and maybe the fall of a spiritual idea that operated in all of our lives whether we knew it consciously or not.

Henry Adams, the turn-of-the-century historian and philosopher, certainly thought so. In 1900, he went to the Paris Exposition where he saw a display of dynamos intended to celebrate the industrial achievements of the last half of the nineteenth century and the glittering promise of technology in the newborn twentieth. Adams was then sixty-two, a curmudgeonly Bostonian, a mistruster of progress, probably a closet Luddite. But he was no fool.

To Adams, the dynamo became a symbol of infinity. As he grew accustomed to the great gallery of machines, he began to feel the forty-foot dynamos as a moral force, much as early Christians felt the Cross.

The earth itself seemed less impressive to him than the power of the dynamo.

Before the end one began to pray to it; inherited instinct taught the natural expression of man before silent and infinite force. Among the thousand symbols of ultimate energy, the dynamo was not so human as some, but it was the most expressive.

He called the dynamo an "occult mechanism"; I would call a steam thresher, a Model T, or a John Deere tractor by the same name. Adams, too, mistrusted the conventional labeling and sequencing of history, but he had a stubborn mind.

He insisted on a relation of sequence, and if he could not reach it by one method, he would try as many methods as science knew. Satisfied that the sequence of men led to nothing and that the sequence of society could lead no further, while the mere sequence of time was artificial and the sequence of thought was chaos, he turned at last to the sequence of force; and thus it happened that, after ten years' pursuit, he found himself lying in the Gallery of Machines at the Great Exposition of 1900, his histori-

1990s: Ghosts in the windbreak

Ghosts of summers past, the rusted hulks of a Case and Hart-Parr tractor sink back into the earth they once plowed. (Photograph by Keith Baum)

cal neck broken by the sudden irruption of forces totally new.

He compares the machine force of the dynamo with the force of the Virgin and Venus in the Middle Ages, here felt only "as sentiment. No American has ever been truly afraid of either." Venus "was goddess because of her force; she was the animated dynamo; she was re-production—the greatest and most mysterious of all energies; all she needed was to be fecund." Fecund indeed . . . how many children of Cyrus McCormick, Henry Ford, John Deere, Charles Dodge, and J. I. Case populate the landscape? We are probably more afraid of power takeoff than of the *ewigliche weibliche* (the eternal feminine). A baler can eat your arm, but a statue is a statue.

The Virgin and Venus in Europe have generated the highest energy ever known to man . . . yet this energy was unknown to the American mind. An American Virgin would never dare command; an American Venus would never dare exist.

What might Adams think of the dashboard Virgins in pious cars, or of the Playmate Venus odor-eater hanging from the mirror of the truck cab? Small reminders of the power of one energy transposed to another? Adams and his friend Saint Gaudens the artist go to look at the Virgin of Amiens near Paris. About this Adams speaks sadly.

St. Gaudens' art was starved from birth, and Adams' instinct was blighted from babyhood. Each of them had but half a nature, and when they came together before the Virgin of Amiens, they ought both to have felt in her the force that made them one, but it was not so . . . Neither of them felt goddesses as power—only as reflected emotion.

Instead "they felt a railway as power."

As Americans, we have tried in this century to make our machinery into Virgin and Venus together, the emblems both of our spiritual and sensual lives, and the true force that holds us together as a culture. Yet it seems to me that, like Adams, we have failed—have grown only "half a nature." How many virginities were lost in a car? How much sexual energy is expended in "laying a little rubber," and goosing the foot feed of a souped-up Pontiac with glass packs in the muffler? How many rites of passage do we undergo in getting our first license, our first car? Why do we name our cars and give them characters, as if they were creatures, or talismans? Turn your radio dial to a country station late at night on a lonesome freeway—you will find the liturgical music of trucks playing for you.

Farming, particularly, has invested not just its trust, but its faith in every religious sense you can imagine into divine machinery. Drive down any township road in farm country during growing season; you will soon find yourself stopped dead behind a tractor or combine the size of a small house covering both lanes. Be-

1980s: Still working

An International Harvester Farmall works the fields in the morning sun. (Photograph by Jerry Irwin)

hind it, like iron octopus tentacles, a plow, drag, or cultivator spreads out over the road shoulder and half the ditch. You will have a long time to drive slowly and admire the force, energy, sheer size and grandeur of that machine. It costs a fortune—likely more than your house and accumulated savings. It is powerful and efficient beyond anything you own. Nature, in some way, is no match for it. It is the gladiator that has conquered manual labor, leaving only the defeat of chance and circumstance. It seems likely to bring even weather under the dominion of its mammoth tires. The farmer who pilots it ("drive" is too timid a word for that iron behemoth), owns a debt that would shock you in its magnitude. You, poor soul, could never borrow that much money! To own that machine requires sacrifice and heroism. It is not a thing but a kind of Grail. Yet, look at the evidence of the countryside with a cold eye. In fifty years, that gargantuan combine will be a rusted ruin, showered by cottonwood fluff in summer and sheathed in ice all winter. When the next behemoth is born that can harvest your beans in forty-five minutes flat, your current behemoth will suddenly become unsalable scrap iron. The heroic steam threshers, plows, tractors, rakes, binders, swathers, grinders, spreaders, balers, cultivators, ad infinitum, of a hundred or even fifty or thirty years ago, sleep silently in the grove, ghosts that have outlived one technical revolution or another, their force spent, their energy leaked out, their dynamos drained.

Those machines were, in some way, false gods. They relieved what Karl Marx called the mindless brutality of rural life, but as in every bargain you sign with Mephistopheles, he wants a price. In the case of farming, the price is debt, overproduction, wasting and depletion of the topsoil, and the necessity for growing large and specialized. Even forty years ago, farming was still a dilettante's pleasure if you wanted it to be—a little of this, a little of that, and a little idling, too, if you were not consumed by greed. A little corn, a little flax, some oats, some hay, some pasture you've never plowed, a hundred chickens, a few ducks, a few milk cows, some feeder cattle, and a leavening of pigs to add charm and fragrance. Large machines put an end to that sort of life. Once you have sunk money into the machinery, you must use it efficiently, or you will soon be farming on the Henry Thoreau model with a hoe in a borrowed garden. There is some question about who owns whom, or who is whose servant: you or your machine? Who gives orders, and who expects to be obeyed? If we give force and energy not to Venus or the Virgin, but to the dynamo, it will ask us some obeisance in return.

But a part of us venerates those old machines, as if they were saints' relics in old churches. The Midwest in the summertime is full of threshing bees and old machinery shows where lovingly preserved or restored equipment is started up, allowed to deafen and delight an audience with its noise and thunder—the putt-putt-putting of the gods—and then paraded down the main street to be admired. "Now *that* was a tractor," says the old codger in the crisp new bib overalls, as the 1915 J. I. Case three-wheeled 1020 model with the four-cylinder vertical engine booms and clanks by on its iron wheels. He has seen a mystery, in every sense of that word—a mystery that once had true force as Adams understood it, and that mystery has brought the old codger joy. What more can you ask of a relic?

I grew up on a farm in the forties already decorated with dead machines, and still farmed, in the opinion of many neighbors, by machines my father should have allowed to die natural deaths long before. He taught me to drive a tractor on a Farmall whose only concession to modernity was rubber tires to replace the old steel spokes. He had spotted his son early as an incompetent, and the old Farmall was, in his opinion, the only tractor on the place slow, heavy, and untippable enough to be proof against my addle-headedness. He was right; I never managed to tip it. Its turtle speed and mechanical unreliability assured my escape from work that had to be done quickly or well. For this, I was grateful.

My father was also a Luddite—I come by it genetically—and no lover of solitary work that interfered with his social pleasures: card playing, story telling, and a little whiskey. The horses were gone by the time my memory begins at the end of World War II, but I heard a wonderful story from my father's hired man from the early forties. According to Ralph, my father preferred horses to tractors and always loudly maintained that together with his team he could do more work than any damn-fool newfangled tractor. He bought one anyway, and sent Ralph east on the tractor while he took the horses west. They used to place small bets on who could plow the most acres in a day. The horses were by this time well past their prime, though my father refused to send them off to the rendering works. Ralph invariably won the bets, and by 1945, the horses had disappeared into legend and probably glue. I asked Ralph why my father, no lover of labor for its own sake, clung to his horses for so long. "He liked them because they knew him," Ralph said, "and besides, he always figured you couldn't scratch a tractor's nose or feed it sugar." My father seemed to have miraculously preserved the half of his nature that Henry Adams thought lost in Americans. I didn't appreciate it enough as a boy, so I owe him some praise now.

What is true of our faith in farm machinery in the Midwest is true of cars over the whole country. It's no longer safe in America to make generalizations about gender, but I'll make one anyway. I think even humorless ideologues might have a hard time finding fault with it. Ask an American man to name the cars he has owned, and to characterize them and describe their peculiarities. Then ask him the same question about human beings he has made love with. The first answer will be richer in detail, affection, and accuracy, and the answer to the second query might even lead back to more detail on the first. Touché, Mr. Adams. I offer no comment on this phenomenon except that it describes something about us that might cause some psychic difficulties. Our real Venus rides not in the front seat but under the hood; our virgin sits not on the dashboard but instead keeps the pistons company.

Whatever else failed in this century, the automobile triumphed. No use questioning its victory. There are more of them than of us, and we design our cities not for our convenience, but for theirs. A rise in the price of meat or grain has no serious political consequences, but double the price of car food: Regimes topple and careers collapse. Their graveyards are a little uglier than ours, stuck in a worse neighborhood maybe, but what can we expect? They are bigger and stronger than we are, and their bodies contain less water so they decompose more slowly. As we see the cars of our youth, in my case, the classic '57 Chevy, the '59 Cadillac with the big fins, the failed Edsel, the disappeared DeSoto, they remind us of our own aging. They are not so sensitive to us, though, and speed by our graveyards without a second glance from the headlights or even a small trembling of the hood ornament.

But Americans, of course, love a winner. Almost everyone is dead who might have a memory of America without paved roads snaking even into rela-

1928 John Deere Model C

Deere & Company's Model C was a famous tractor of its day, yet it's also a tractor that hardly exists today. Created as Deere's secret weapon in the war against the Farmall, the C was introduced in 1928—and went out of production that same year after only 110 were built. Deere feared that dealers would confuse the name over the telephone with its Model D, so the C was slightly revised and re-introduced later in 1928 as the Model GP. Owners: Walter and Bruce Keller of Kaukauna, Wisconsin. (Photograph by Andrew Morland)

tive wilderness, gas stations (now convenience stores) numberless as stars, and traffic jams in the middle of nowhere. We *are* our cars or our pickups—a Buick is something to believe in, Ford has a better idea, what's good for General Motors is good for us. Our driver's license is our national identity card, our certification of adulthood and citizenship. We pray in our cars, make love in them, bank in them, eat in them, glory in them. What we have not quite figured out is what to do with them when they die.

On farms we keep them, put them in an out-of-the-way spot, and let them be. Sometimes, as age overtakes them, they become beautiful and we photograph them by moonlight, lonesome half-wrecked machines with metal eye sockets and wrinkled fenders. The old red truck is our version of the equestrian statue or the monumental arch. We nod as we pass by to do chores, and remember good times and close scrapes. We measure our lives by their progress at sinking into the topsoil to wait for the next glacier. Phebe Hanson grew up in a Norwegian parsonage in Sacred Heart, Minnesota, in the thirties. In this poem, she remembers waiting in a neighbor's grove while her mother lay dying of TB. These cars seem likely to outwait even the glacier, biding their time until the second coming.

COTTONWOODS

In the cottonwood grove
behind Dahl's farm
the eyes of nesting cars
stare at me before
I crawl into them,
pretend I am driving;
power flows from the wheels,

I believe I am in control,
forget my mother's heart
lies fading in the little bedroom
beyond the rows of corn.

They have sent me away
from her dying to play in the grove,
to sit in old cars,
to whisper into the ears of corn,
towering above me as I sit between the rows
reading her letters

which say she misses me,
even though it is quieter without me
and my brother fighting.
He has brought her a goldfish
from the little pond
beside the pergola house
and laid it on her stomach.

Years later I return to the grove,
where the cottonwood trees
have grown scrawny,
but the old cars are still there,
their eyes stare at me,
unseeing and dead.

Sometimes we love cars enough to bring them back to life. Gordon Brekken, the father of a friend of mine, collects Studebakers and restores them. For him, a Studebaker is not only a car, but a moral and aesthetic choice—a touchstone by which we judge beauty and good sense. He adorns his everyday cars (alas, no longer Studebakers!) with a bumper sticker: "Keep America Beautiful. Drive a Studebaker." His farm shed is half full, not of practical machinery, but of old Studebakers in various stages of repair. He covers them with plastic to protect them from dust and cold. He studies classified ads for Studebaker parts and keeps his eyes attentive when he drives by junk yards. He subscribes to *Studebaker* magazine, reads it faithfully, and drives long distances to Studebaker rallies to show his cars in competition and "talk Studebaker" with those who have risen to moral consciousness. I once told him about a junked pink Studebaker I discovered behind a bar in Bozeman, Montana. He wanted to know the model, the year, and a rough parts inventory, and grumbled at my foolishness when I couldn't provide them. Americans, as Henry Adams knew, take force seriously even when they don't find it in old cathedrals. Adams says that "all the steam in the world could not, like the Virgin, build Chartres," but it built Studebakers and that, as my friend's father might say, is something not too bad. Even if we don't build the Cathedral of Chartres, we need the courage to love what we do build. Here's the American question: Why can't God be as easily manifest in a Studebaker as in a statue?

My cousin, Daren Gislason, gardens with the same passion and intensity as my friend's father collects and

1937 Case CC Special
This high-clearance version of Case's renowned Model CC was designed for use on sugar cane operations. Introduced in 1929, the various versions of the CC continued in production for a full decade. Owner: Charles English Sr., of Evansville, Indiana. (Photograph by Ralph W. Sanders)

cherishes Studebakers. He appropriated land from neighborhood farmers along the Yellow Medicine river, and made a garden the size of Versailles, miles of trails through boxelders, willows, and unplowed prairie, decorated with beds of iris, tulips, marigolds, wild flowers, native grasses and bushes, God's plenty of flora. He collects the junk of Minneota to recycle in his garden. Every hundred yards there's an old couch or a chair, half decomposed but still serviceable, where strollers can take a rest and contemplate virgins, dynamos, Studebakers, or whatever else is on their minds. About fifteen years ago, unknown neighborhood wags decided to play a practical joke on him. They hauled the corpse of a black '39 Plymouth seven miles north of town and plopped it in the middle of his garden.

He remained calm; he's a man who understands the Zen of gardens and accepts the unusual gifts of the universe on their own terms. He planted bluebells on the hood and windshield, started a native cactus garden on the black roof; installed raspberry bushes behind the trunk, and used the interior to store hoes, rakes, spades, pails, and birdseed. Within a few years, the old Plymouth was transformed from nature into art—witty recycling, the only sort that matters. Visitors came to be photographed with their foot mounted on the fine and still intact old running boards, yellow cactus blooming behind their hair.

The cactus perished in a wet year, but by then native prairie had almost overwhelmed the Plymouth. It has turned into a black iron ghost being eaten by grass, a fine metaphor and still a much-loved prop for local photographers. Hailstorms broke out a window or two, but the front seat still provides a happy home for garden tools. This Plymouth is junk transformed by love and a sense of humor into something like a shrine. Only a fool would try to answer the question: To what? I don't know, and neither do you.

In Alliance, Nebraska, dead cars have been consciously transformed into a shrine. Carhenge is a replica of Stonehenge, the old Druid shrine in England, but here built not from rock but from everything from a '58 Cadillac to a '79 Honda—all painted stony gray to resemble their ancient namesake. As in Lourdes or Canterbury, you can buy postcards, tee shirts, and bric-a-brac at Carhenge. Imagine Henry Adams, now three-quarters of a century dead, reincarnated to visit Alliance, Nebraska. What might he feel? Adams "complained that the power embodied in a railway train" (he might have updated that to a Cadillac . . .) "could never be embodied in art." Adams had, of course, seen the real Stonehenge, one of the oldest sights of force, energy, emotion in Europe. Would he have laughed at this kitschy imitation of spiritual power? Would he have thought Carhenge a poor try at restoring the lost half of his nature? He would have been both right and wrong: right in that Carhenge, of course, is pure kitsch, a joke at the expense of the Druids. It requires no genius to understand that.

And yet . . . and yet . . . the builders of Carhenge made better than they knew. If indeed we live in a century that has worshipped machines, technology, a better mousetrap for a better universe, then we live also in a century that has seen incontrovertible evidence of the failure of all those machines: the car, the steam engine, the hydrogen bomb, the personal computer, and the cuisinart. Our gods don't work. Probably the last generations of them didn't either. But just as we honor J. S. Bach, Søren Kierkegaard, Thomas Aquinas, the unnamed architect of Chartres, Silbermann the organ builder, and the anonymous crafters of windows, so do we owe the Cadillac and the John Deere a little honor, too. All of them gave us energy—humor, intelligence, beauty, force (to use Adams' word), and if the energy has leaked out of them a little now, it's time for us as humans to imagine a new force. Meanwhile, something worth a look is decaying in the grove behind the barn if our eyes are open to see it.

1940 Silver King

The Fate-Root-Heath Company of Plymouth, Ohio, began as a builder of steam railroad locomotives before venturing into the tractor field in 1933. Silver Kings were never prolific in the fields, but their owners believed in them, and many have been lovingly restored. Owner: Perry Jennings of Decatur, Tennessee. (Photograph by Ralph W. Sanders)

Romancing the Rust: Roger's Metaphysical Examination into the Whys and Wherefores of Tractor Restoration

By Roger Welsch

Roger Welsch is a farm tractor poet, philosopher, and paleontologist all rolled into one.

He is also a high priest of the vintage tractor world, spreading the good word about tractors far and wide. During his stint as a television personality on CBS TV's *Sunday Morning*, Roger showcased tractors whenever he could. His writings on tractors appear regularly in *Successful Farming*'s "Ageless Iron" section, as well as in *Esquire*, *Smithsonian*, and *Nebraska Farmer*. In addition, he is the author of more than twenty books, including *Old Tractors and the Men Who Love Them* and *Busted Tractors and Rusty Knuckles*. As John Carter of the Nebraska State Historical Society noted, "We all knew sooner or later that Roger would write a book about religion."

In this article ripe with its sage philosphy, Roger examines why we restore old iron.

One of the toughest tractor questions I have ever had to deal with came from my beloved wife, Lovely Linda, as she viewed the completion of one of my projects: "What are you going to do with it?"

I had been working in my shop on a battered old Allis-Chalmers WC tractor for more than two years. When it was dragged out of the woodlot where it had begun to rust and rot right into the soil right where it sat, the motor was stuck, the magneto and carburetor were missing, there were no tires and not much by way of wheels. About the most that could be said of this wreck is that it was still recognizable as an Allis-Chalmers WC tractor, circa 1937.

In my shop, I cleaned the old wreck until it was possible to lean on it without needing a bath. I completely dismantled it. I repaired parts, replaced parts, restored parts. Slowly, carefully, lovingly, I worked on that tractor. Day after day Linda watched me return to the house, sometimes in victory, sometimes in defeat—dirty, bloody, burned, bruised, sore in every muscle.

And she was in the yard when my buddies Dan, Bondo, and Melvin came by that wonderful day to help

1959 Allis-Chalmers D10
A gloriously restored Allis D10, the apple of many a farmer's eye. Owner: Little Britain Ag Supply of Little Britain, Pennsylvania. (Photograph by Keith Baum)

me roll that tractor out of the shop, adjust the carb and mag, and—what a moment!—turn the crank. She watched as grown men danced and cheered and poured beer over each other when the tractor belched an ugly black cloud, spewed water and oil from various orifices, snorted, belched . . . and then roared that distinct, wonderful snarl of the unmuffled Allis WC.

Later that same night, as I sat in our living room, cleaned up but still grinning, she asked me the question: "What are you going to do with it?"

I was utterly stymied by her query. Hmmm. "You know," I had to admit, "I have no idea."

And I didn't. Frankly, I hadn't even thought about where I would park the tractor, much yet what to *do* with it. All the time, money, effort, love, and frustration I'd spent on that machine ultimately didn't have anything to do with the result, a running tractor. As I considered Linda's very reasonable query, I came to understand a lot more about myself and my passion with working with old tractors: It was not so much the last moment of the tractor's repair—that instant it started and ran—that was important. Not at all. Repairing and rebuilding that machine was about . . . well, repairing and rebuilding that machine. It was a matter of process, not item, a journey of getting there rather than being there. Now that the tractor was running and rolling . . . well, in my mind there just wasn't much fun left in it for me.

Ultimately, almost perfunctorily, I donated the tractor to the new tractor museum in Lincoln, Nebraska, at the site of the revered, internationally famed University of Nebraska tractor test facility. They raffled it off and made a few thousand dollars which they used to restore other tractors in their exhibits. It was won, as fate would have it, by a Nebraska woman who, after we had sold raffle tickets for more than a year all over the nation, turned out to have purchased her ticket the morning of the drawing!

Well, all of that was interesting, and a lot of fun, and a worthwhile thing to do with an old friend I had nursed back to health. After all that time in the shop, that tractor *had* almost become a member of the family. Believe it or not, Linda actually shed a tear when they came to haul the tractor away.

Not me. My heart wasn't in the tractor as she stood there, proudly running again after having been abandoned for dead. Yes, I felt a certain amount of pride, even though she still looked pretty shabby next to other

1935 Minneapolis-Moline Twin City Model J
When Minneapolis-Moline was formed in a merger in 1929, the fledgling company inherited the stalwart Twin City line of tractors. In 1934, the new firm released the Twin City Model J, a thoroughly modern machine for its day. The J line would continue in production until 1938, but its heritage lived on in the Z and R Series that ended production in 1956. Owner: Dale Nafe of Pierson, Iowa. (Photograph by Ralph W. Sanders)

machines that have been brought back to factory newness, while my tractor had only gone through a transformation from "scrap metal" to "running tractor." But my thoughts were not on what had been done, this finished result. No, my aim was on the tractor I was planning on rolling—or more precisely, dragging—into my shop next.

I was so excited about *that* prospect that I was salivating at the very idea of cleaning parts, checking innards, long days in a warm shop with snow flying against my windows, conversations with more mechanically experienced pals about gears, rods, rings, and stuck parts. . . . What Linda and others saw as a real mess was to me a barrel of delights. And once again, the thought of what to do with it once it was running again was inconsequential compared to the delights I anticipated in *getting* it running!

That, to me, is the heart of tractor repair and restoration. A lot of the folks who deal with machinery, men and women used to the violence and reality of wrenches, sledges, cheaters, prybars, pullers, and breaker bars might not be comfortable with a warm and fuzzy word like "romance" but that *is* the word. For many of us, perhaps most of us, this old tractor thing is more a matter of mind than muscle, more of satisfaction than profit, more of the heart than iron.

1951 Massey-Harris 44 Diesel

Above: *Massey-Harris's first new tractor design following World War II rolled onto Canadian farms in 1946 as the Model 44. It was followed two years later in 1948 by this 44 Diesel version. The 44 repaid their owners' investments manyfold over the years, and the model continued in production in revised versions until 1958. Owner: Dan Peterman of Webster City, Iowa. (Photograph by Ralph W. Sanders)*

1980s: Tricky work

Facing page: *A farm youth carefully steers his trusty Farmall Cub to back a wagonload of eggs into position at a roadside stand. (Photograph by Jerry Irwin)*

History in the Barn

It was while doing the morning chores that we came upon the tractor in the barn. I was tagging along with my friend, David Benson, helping him with his chores, but more often than not simply chatting and gabbing as he played the tour guide, showing off his eclectic collection of machinery as we made the rounds of his farm in southwestern Minnesota. It was a typical autumn day in that part of the country—which is to say, the kind of glorious, clear, cool, sunny day that made farmwork a joy.

Now, my friend's farm was not your typical farm. There was not your usual modern Ford or Kubota tractor parked in the machine shed, nor your Ford and Chevrolet pickup truck pulled up in front of the house.

Things operated different here.

My friend's farm led a secret second life as a kind of orphanage for mechanical foundlings, a safe house for wayward technology, a retirement home for obsolete engineering, and a last resort for unwanted machinery. And the farm was surrounded by windbreaks that protected the home place from the westerly winds, but also served as a graveyard for old tractors, trucks, and implements that seemed to not truly be dead but simply waiting to be resurrected once again.

Let me explain further.

In the barn, next to a handful of dairy cows, were stables for two Percheron workhorses. And these gentle giants, a mother and her daughter, still worked, pulling manure spreaders, hay wagons, and a rock-gathering flatbed in the fields. A small herd of sheep, a gaggle of geese, and a flock of chickens lived in other outbuildings, sheds, and henhouses. With the mix of crops, this seemed like your typical 1930s family farm—albeit transported by a time machine smack dab into the 1990s.

But it was the choice of machinery that truly set my friend's farm apart. The son of Swedish immigrants, who at that time still lived on the homeplace, my friend had inherited a love and fascination for equipment that originated from far-flung shores.

With his Swedish heritage it should come as little shock that he was enamored with Volvo automobiles. Yet this love affair with the Swedish car went beyond simple transportation needs. On the farm at any one time may be a gaggle of Volvo sedans, coupes, and sports cars ranging in vintage over a spectrum of four decades of age from the 1950s through the 1980s. The favored setup was naturally Volvo's famous station wagon, which due to its heavy-duty clutch and shock absorbers, capable chassis, high-output heater, and huge wagon bed, made it ideal to serve double duty in the farm's fields for walking soybeans, picking rocks, mending fence, and any other sundry chore. The only thing the station wagons lacked in comparison with your typical Ford pickup truck was four-wheel drive.

Now it might seem odd to use a fleet of Volvo station wagons as general-purpose farm pickup trucks—sort of like using a goat for a lawn mower. But when you reconsidered, Willys' Jeep and the Land-Rover were offered after World War II with plows and other specially built farm implements, so why not? If my friend chose Volvo station wagons instead of the tried-and-true Ford or Chevy pickup truck, well, that was his choice.

1930s: History in the barn
Working beneath tobacco leaves hung out to dry in the barn rafters overhead, a farmer applies oil to the transmission of his John Deere Model D before sending it back into the field. (Photograph by J. C. Allen & Son)

The thing is, those Volvos shared valuable machinery shed space with a virtual museum of ancient motorcycles. On first glance, these cycles seemed to be collected and curated to display the complex variety of cycles that were created in all corners of the globe. But as you made the rounds with my friend and heard each cycle's story, you understood that there was *meaning* to their existence on the farm. A duo of 1960s Triumph vertical twins, for instance, had a favored place in a shed, as they also shared a favored place in my friend's memory: He had bought these cycles with an acquaintance in England during a college-years grand tour of Europe. The Triumphs came home with them and served time on the farm for everything from herding stock to quick-and-dirty gofer transportation.

Near the Triumphs was parked an English-built Ariel single; other American and European steeds stood in the shadows, too covered by the dust of the years to differentiate the brands without the aid of a cleaning rag and, sometimes, a magnifying glass to examine the worn decals or emblems on the tanks. Another shed contained a bevy of BMWs of different ages and configurations, which was another favored brand as a BMW R26 single had carried my friend and his soon-to-be-wife on a tour of the Baja Peninsula also during their college days. A 1950s German-made NSU 500-cc single waited out its time on this earth in a stable nearby, while my friend shook his head over a rare Velocette thumper that he had just missed out on at a neighboring farm auction. He probably had plans to pull stumps with it or something.

But it was in the wide and varied selection of farm tractors that my friend truly excelled. The casual observer practically needed a pocket-sized field guide to tractors to keep tabs on the variety of machines as you strolled the acreage. Fortunately, I had my friend as tour guide on this fine fall morning.

We walked by a John Deere Model A that was waiting patiently in the center of the farmyard to do its chores. The choice of a Johnny Popper was nothing out of the ordinary, but its vintage and story were: My friend's dad had bought this A brand new in 1951 and used it throughout his farming career; my friend still had it and used it regularly. This was no coddled and polished showpiece—although after it's lifetime of hard farm labor, it probably deserved to be.

The Model A shared chores with two other green machines bearing the yellow deer insignia: a 1939 Model B and a 1949 Model R. The R had been purchased from a retired neighbor, who had bought the diesel new; his daughter now was interested in buying it back as she had fond memories of plowing with her dad's old Deere. Another Model R hibernated behind some outbuildings, where it donated its components as a parts tractor to keep the '49 R alive and well.

My friend's favored mounts—at the moment at least—were two David Brown tractors, which hailed from Great Britain. The David Brown concern's history stretched back to 1860 when it made gears for early mechanical contrivances. In 1936, Brown joined forces with Irishman Harry Ferguson to build their short-lived Ferguson-Brown Model A. Ferguson soon left for greener pastures and a handshake agreement with Henry Ford to produce the famed Ford-Ferguson N Series. Brown soldiered on with tractors of his own, which became cousins to another of Brown's ventures: hand-crafting the glorious Aston Martin and Lagonda automobiles. The machines that had somehow immigrated to this Minnesota farmstead were a 1960s Model 880 and 990; a third David Brown slumbered in the windbreak.

Sharing a shed with the David Browns were two 1970s Deutz air-cooled diesel tractors, which were growing in popularity on this farm at the moment. These machines hailed from Germany, where the Deutz firm boasted a proud history. In 1907, Deutz was the pioneer builder of tractors powered by the fledgling four-cycle internal-combustion engine. Deutz's *Pfuglokomotive*, or "Plow-locomotive," was a massive 3-ton affair featuring a 25-horsepower gas-fueled engine.

In addition to the working machines, a mishmash of obsolete but ageless iron rested their bones in the windbreak, ancient American machines that were built by farsighted entrepreneurs in the early days of the tractor. The names cast into the radiators were grown over by the prairie grasses, grasses that these tractors had once turned over while breaking the virgin land. Trees—some of them perhaps two decades old—had grown up through open areas of the tractor chassis.

Now, this was far more horsepower than a small family farm required, but obviously that was not the point of having all of these tractors and other machines. My friend harbored a fascination for these machines that transcended the need to plant oats and cut hay.

1990s: "Barnyard Buddies"

With a John Deere tractor built from a green-painted mailbox, a trio of farm youths dream of the day they will be old enough to pilot Pa's Deere Model A. Iowa artist Charles Freitag painted this nostalgic image of old times on the farm. (Apple Creek Publishing)

Thus, it should have come as little surprise to me on this beautiful fall day when we came upon yet another tractor in yet another barn.

This tractor, however, was truly special. It sat in a far-flung shed that had once held animal stables but now was filled with all of the other unrecognizable and incomplete bits of machinery that a farm accumulates over the years. The tractor was lost in the shadows of the small barn but as we entered, light from the doorway cast a golden glow over the old machine that to any lover of old machines would have been indistinguishable from a halo. My friend simply stood in the doorway, regarding this last tractor fondly and allowing me a moment of discovery.

I walked into the barn as if I was walking into a sepulcher, stirring up motes of dust and dry hay with each footstep. I moved around the cobweb-covered tractor with reverence, not daring to touch it.

The tractor was a John Deere D. It was a 1927 model, as my friend told me.

For some reason, we were speaking with almost hushed voices.

I continued to circle the machine, admiring its straightforward design, a design that was purely functional with none of the streamlining that Henry Dreyfuss would later add to the Deeres. The wheels were bare iron cleats and the seat was a solid cast saddle. This was a machine for working.

As any tractor enthusiast worth his or her salt knows, the Model D is one of the most famous farm tractors ever. The D also holds the record for the longest production run of any American tractor, being built from 1923 to 1953—a thirty-year run that is challenged only by Farmall's Cub at twenty-eight years. The D was the first tractor on many American farms, the mechanical mule that replaced the horses, the machine that broke the prairie sod, the tractor that helped provide food for a growing nation. During its day, some 160,000 Model D tractors were built, a testament to its capabilities and the respect farmers held for this

1949 International Harvester Farmall Cub

The Farmall Cub was second only to the great John Deere Model D in longevity of production. Produced from 1947 to 1975, the Cub was the apple of its owner's eye on the garden farm, vegetable operation, golf course fairway, and just about anywhere else a small tractor was needed. Owner: Lawrence Shaw of Gainesville, Florida. (Photograph by Ralph W. Sanders)

1918 Samson Sieve-Grip

Above: *After witnessing Henry Ford's success with the Fordson tractor, arch-rival General Motors of Pontiac, Michigan, suffered a bad case of corporate envy and ached to get into the farming field. Instead of going the laborious route of developing its own tractor, GM simply purchased the Samson Tractor Works of Stockton, California, in 1918, and placed its hopes on the firm's bizarre Sieve-Grip tractor. The Sieve-Grip might have worked well in the wet soil of California's Central Valley, but it was almost exactly the wrong tractor for all other farmers. GM quickly withdrew the fabulous machine and built a Fordson copy in the form of the Samson Model M, but it too never found success. Owner: Fred Heidrick of Woodland, California. (Photograph by Ralph W. Sanders)*

1953 John Deere Model R

Right: *Deere & Company planned to re-place its flagship Model D in 1949 with the new Model R, but the D's footsteps were large ones to fill. While the R found a strong market for its diesel engine, there were still many believers in the good old D, and it was not until 1953 that the classic Johnny Popper ended production. Owner: David Walker of Chillicothe, Missouri. (Photograph by Ralph W. Sanders)*

simple machine.

What's this D's history, I asked, sort of like one would ask after the bloodlines of a thoroughbred race horse.

My friend had also fallen under the spell of the tractor, so it was a moment before he could shift gears to relate the story.

It was the autumn of 1966, and my friend was working at the tractor salvageyard south of Worthington, Minnesota, saving money to go off to college. This salvageyard was one of the largest anywhere. It bore a collection of tractors, implements, and combines that were sorted by color—and hence by make—into rows that stretched away to the horizon, undulating over the rolling hillsides. From the distance, the salvageyard glowed like fields of some rare, beautiful flowers: a section of red tulips, maybe; another of bright green neighbored patches of gold, light blue, orange, and more. Yet the red was Farmall Red, the green was Deere Green, the gold was Minneapolis-Moline's trademark Prairie Gold, the blue was Ford Blue, the orange Case's Flambeau Red—every color farm tractors were ever painted. At sunset, with the prairie light reflecting off of the ancient sheetmetal, it was truly a gorgeous sight.

My friend was finishing up his employment at the yard before leaving for college when one day this 1927 Deere Model D appeared. It was complete, which was a rare thing for a tractor this old. It had been hauled in from a farm somewhere in Nebraska, just one more piece of obsolete machinery. By chance or by luck, this D had not been melted down as part of the scrap metal drive during World War II. Now, in 1966, however, it was really too old to add to the salvageyard inventory: No one was still using such an ancient machine and would ever want parts. So, this D was destined to be junked out.

My friend caught sight of the D, and something about this decades-old piece of farming history spoke to him, a teenager. He hustled in to talk to the owner of the salvageyard and begged him not to junk out the tractor. The owner may have sensed the history of this particular machine, but old tractors were just old tractors in the 1960s, and business was always business. The machine was going to be junked.

My friend thought quickly. He offered a bargain: He would work to buy the D. And so a deal was struck. My friend labored an extra week for no pay, and when the week was up, the old D was his.

He got the D home to his parents' farm, parked it in the barn, and left for college. The D had sat here ever since.

Now, twenty-some years later, we both stood silently for a while, staring at the tractor. I suppose he was thinking of old days and the way things once were. I was mesmerized by the story: A youth on his way to college and a tractor that was saved from the dustbins of history. But it was even more than that: This tractor *was* history itself.

After we had gotten our fill of gazing at the venerable old D, we gathered up our gear and set off doing chores again. But there was one chore still to do in this barn, part of my friend's typical rounds. Many of the cars, cycles, and tractors on his farm he used—if not daily, well, at least once a month or so. Other machines he just let sit. Some he had good intentions or dreams of getting around to fixing while their parts rusted as solid as the original lump of iron ore from which they were made. A single person simply couldn't keep all of these machines among the living. But the D was special, something separate and apart from all of the other machines on the farm. And this gave it a place in his chores, along with feeding the chickens, tending to the drafthorses, and milking the cows. Whenever his farm work brought him by this barn, he stopped for a moment, opened the old doors, went inside to the D, and grasped its solid flywheel with both of his hands, leaned into it with his weight, and turned the flywheel so that the D's crankshaft and rods and pistons and all of the rest of its engine would never seize up.

1953 International Harvester Farmall Super H

Hiding behind the rusted carcass of an old Farmall, this restored Super H carries on the legacy. Owner: Kevin Haarklan of Dane, Wisconsin. (Photograph by Andy Kraushaar)

"For a better living and a better world through lower production costs and increased profits for the farmer, less world unrest from hunger and want, greater security for world peace."
—Ferguson tractor advertisement, 1949